HARROGATE
1849

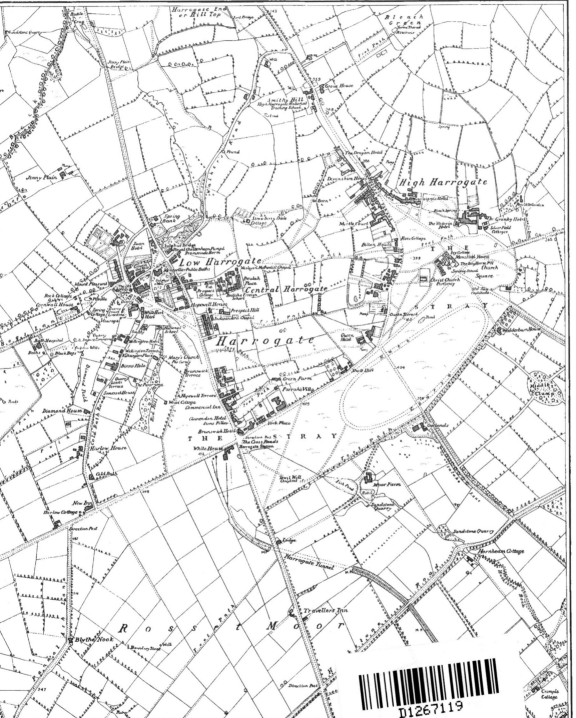

Map YORKSHIRE 154 Surveyed in 1849 by Capt. Tucker R.E.

Scale 1:7500

0   200   400   600   800   1000 yards

HARROGATE
PAST

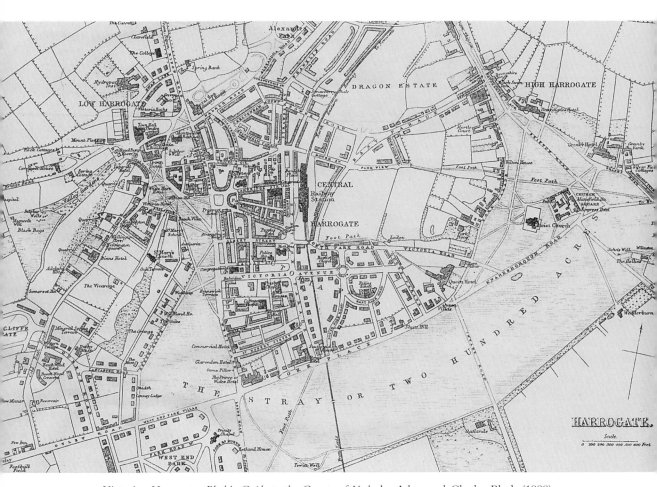

Victorian Harrogate. *Black's Guide to the County of York*, by Adam and Charles Black (1888).

HARROGATE
PAST

W. R. Mitchell

Phillimore

2001

Published by
PHILLIMORE & CO. LTD.
Shopwyke Manor Barn, Chichester, West Sussex

ISBN 1 86077 181 5

Printed and bound in Great Britain by
BIDDLES LTD.
Guildford, Surrey

Contents

For Gillian
and
Roger Oldfield

List of Illustrations

Frontispiece: Victorian Harrogate, 1888

Illustration Acknowledgements

I would like to thank the following for the loan of the pictures: Bettys Café Tearooms, 17; Cabinet Album Views of Harrogate and Knaresborough (printed in Germany) 1, 13, 21, 36, 38, 39, 41, 47, 61, 63, 86, 87, 103, 118, 123; Harrogate Advertiser, 77; Harrogate Museums and Arts, Royal Pump Room Museum, 34, 44, 50, 64, 66, 69, 156; David Joy, 56-8; the Malcolm Neesam Collection, 26, 79, 80, 132, 134; North Yorkshire County Library, 5, 6, 10, 11, 19, 22, 27-30, 33, 51, 60, 68, 70-3, 82, 83, 89, 92, 93, 96, 98-100, 104, 112, 116, 120, 125 126, 128, 133, 149, 150; Bertram Unne Collection, 35, 153; Yorkshire Archaeological Society, 4, 9, 14, 31, 101, 105, 106, 141; Yorkshire Post, 59, 108-110, 114, 115, 137, 138, 147, 148, 152, 154.

Acknowledgements

My first real introduction to Harrogate came through Bertram Unne (1913-81), who was a native of Newcastle but of Swedish descent. He settled in Harrogate as a photographer and continued a tradition of pictorial records that had begun in Victorian times, as well as recording rural life in all parts of the county. He was ever-ready to talk about the town that had adopted him. I was happy to learn that, with grants from the Victoria and Albert Museum and the British Library, his collection of negatives had been acquired by the North Yorkshire County Library and is in safe custody at Northallerton.

In my quest for information I have, of course, quarried for facts about the spa town in the standard histories. Of special value has been *A History of Harrogate and Knaresborough*, the product of eight years' research undertaken by two university tutorial classes under the direction of Bernard Jennings. After its publication in 1970, few facets of local life remained unexplained. Asa Briggs, who wrote the foreword, especially liked an inscription that was drafted in 1743 when a subscription was being raised in Harrogate to provide the town with a church: 'To the glory of God and the good of Mankind more Especially of the inhabitants of Harrowgate with Bilton.'

A pleasant editorial job that fell to me at the Dalesman Publishing Company in 1954 was preparing for the press W. Haythornthwaite's *Harrogate Story*. Though it was later revealed to contain a few inaccuracies and significant omissions—as is the way with pioneering histories—the author had made a bold attempt to trace the evolution of Harrogate in its middle years, from Georgian village to Victorian town. The researches of Malcolm G. Neesam, the Harrogate historian, have put much flesh on the bare bones of Harrogate history. His weekly feature in the *Harrogate Advertiser* has a wide following. He was especially kind to me some years ago when I was researching the Dales associations of the composer Edward Elgar. He renewed that help during the preparation of this latest volume.

I am indebted to Dr. Arnold Kellett, of Knaresborough, who has an exhaustive knowledge of the district and who added one more task to many in hand when he agreed to read through a draft of this book and make comments—this at a time when he was still recovering from a serious illness. Maurice Baren, a native of the town and the author of well-illustrated books on Yorkshire business enterprises, loaned me books from his well-stocked shelves. Officials of Harrogate Borough Council have shown interest in my project and have responded promptly to my enquiries.

Chapter One

An Overview

Encompassing a total of 515 square miles, the Harrogate District of North Yorkshire extends from the head of Nidderdale, where a glacier-hewn valley is flanked by heather moors, eastwards to Marston Moor, on the Plain of York, the fatty heartland of the county. The town is an upstart compared with the much earlier settlement of Knaresborough, which is perched beside the Nidd gorge and was a busy town, complete with church and castle, when High and Low Haregate were modest settlements in ancient forest. Situated on the magnesian limestone belt, Knaresborough was built of a light grey stone distinct from the brown gritstone of Harrogate (the use of bricks on a large scale only following the arrival of the railway in 1848). The soil around Knaresborough was light and workable. Harrogate lay in an area of clay, the exploitation of which had to await the arrival of the Anglians with their oxen and heavy ploughs.

1   An engraving of Knaresborough and the River Ure.

2 Knaresborough and the River Ure.

The Harrogate District encompasses Ripon, which despite its relatively small size has city status. Its cathedral is over thirteen centuries old. At Ripon, a hornblower nightly 'sets the watch', as his many predecessors have done for well over a thousand years. Markenfield Hall, a fortified, moated manor on high ground between the city and Ripley, has been owned by only three families, the Markenfields, Egertons and Grantleys, since the 14th century. Where roads from Harrogate and Knaresborough meet, a few miles from town, stands Ripley Castle, ancestral home of the Ingilby family, whose ancient links with Harrogate included being among the 27 individuals with rights of pasturage on Harrogate's Stray when this huge tract of open ground was granted for public use in 1778. James I stayed at Ripley Castle in 1603, an interlude in his journey from Scotland to London, when he claimed the English throne.

When, on my first visit to Harrogate many years ago, a local man claimed that the town stands at the centre of Britain, I was prepared to accept this as an expression of local pride. He explained that the town stands some 400 miles from Lands End and 400 miles from John o' Groats, about 200 miles from London and a similar distance from Edinburgh. It is located half way between east and west coasts. It is also a 'gateway' to the Yorkshire Dales National Park, though the handiest major valley, which

3   A watering point, Ripley, is surmounted by a stone representation of wild boar.

4   A Victorian study of Ripley Castle, near Harrogate. The Ingilby family, who lived here for many centuries, were important local landowners.

5   Birk Crag.

6   Crag House, Birk Crag.

is Nidderdale, was unaccountably left out of the Park on its designation. The town is in soft, warm gritstone country, to the east of the Pennines, with a few mini-mountains such as Almscliffe Crag and Birk Crag, noted more as vantage points than for their high elevation. It grew up on what was described by Michael Stanhope, a 17th-century chronicler, as a 'rude barren Moore' where there was 'piercing bleake aire'. Thomas Baskerville, another early writer, was captivated by the 'noble prospect' over the vale to the city of York, some eighteen miles away. Daniel Defoe reached Harrogate from Knaresborough and found pleasure in what he saw. Defoe, creator of *Robinson Crusoe*, had been led to believe that this was a desolate, out-of-the-way place and a habitat of men who 'would only retire to it for religious mortifications and to hate the world'. He found it 'quite otherwise'.

In the middle of the 18th century, Smollett described 'Harrowgate' as being 'a wild common, bare, bleak, without tree or shrub or the least kinds of cultivation'. To Sydney Smith, writing some fifty years later, the area was still bleak and unkempt. 'When I saw it, there were only nine mangy fir trees there and even they all leaned away from it.' Edmund Bogg, of Leeds, in a book describing a journey from 'Eden Vale to the Plains of York', reached the 'fairy town of Harrogate which spreads out on the high range of lands, finely situated for receiving the salubrious breezes wafted to its doors from the heather-clad hills.' William Grainge, another Victorian chronicler, described Harrogate as being 'scattered over a piece of lofty table land, along the bottom and up the corresponding slope of a small valley, without much order or regularity of design; yet presenting from all points of view an open, airy, elegant and substantial appearance.'

The 88 mineral springs that were to give Harrogate renown lay in a small area. Generally they were of sulphur or iron, the sulphur imparting a tang that has often been compared with rotten eggs. Sulphur water is a strong purgative, guaranteed to empty quickly the bowels of anyone who drinks a pint or two. The salinity of the springs varied, those known as chalybeate wells yielding iron waters, free of salt.

The Tewit Well at High Harrogate, which was capped in 1971, had been used by the ailing and the obese for four centuries. No one is quite sure where the well lies but the approximate site is denoted by a domed and

7 Tewit Well, built in the classical style and discovered in 1571 by William Slingsby, was the original structure that covered the Old Sulphur Well.

colonnaded rotunda, designed by Thomas Chippindale in 1807 and moved here from the Old Sulphur Well in Low Harrogate. Modern visitors chancing across the rotunda think it must be a classical temple or even a bandstand. It is approached along an avenue of mature trees, which give the path the gloomy aspect of a cathedral aisle; it is shielded by a mature chestnut tree and is within a short distance of the railway. The chatter of a magpie merges with the whine and clatter of a passing diesel train. Tewit Well is said to have been named after the local name for the lapwing, which must have been numerous when, as the presence of springs and pools denotes, the Stray was undeveloped. Those who drank the sulphur water of Harrogate were inclined first to grip their noses as they were assailed by a pungent tang. Ely Hargrove, of Knaresborough, after mentioning the malodorous waters of the well, observed that they were being used 'both externally and internally by all ranks with amazing success'. When Harrogate had been incorporated as a municipal borough in 1884, it took as its motto *Arx Celebris Fontibus*, or 'a citadel famous for its springs'. Here was found a motley throng of invalids, hypochondriacs and those who purported to be able to help them. Charles Dickens, during a lecture tour in 1858, described Harrogate as 'the queerest place, with the strangest people in it, leading the oddest lives'.

The Stray, a feature of which a visitor to Harrogate is always aware, extends as a broad crescent from the Esplanade in Low Harrogate to the *Granby* in High Harrogate, bringing a country flavour to within easy viewing range of the stately ranks of Victorian buildings. Once part of a belt of common land that separated embryo Harrogate from the much older communities of Beckwith and Rossett, the Stray took its present form in the 1770s, when it was declared, with legal support, that it should remain 'ever hereafter open and unenclosed', providing free access to anyone wishing to visit the mineral springs here or to 'drink the waters

there arising and take benefit thereof'. Now it is mainly used for horse riding, for walking or for impromptu games like football. The Stray-gate Proprietors, who were awarded rights to pasture stock, controlled in all 215 acres, an additional 15 being made up of bits and pieces of land at the sides of roads. Whereas now the folk of Harrogate object strongly if planners propose to modify the Stray by as much as an inch, the old-time Proprietors were charged with improving the Stray, which was marshy and adorned by gorse bushes. The ground was levelled and trees were planted for 'shelter and ornament'. An Act of 1841 replaced the somewhat lethargic Proprietors with Commissioners, charged with the improvement of the town. They did not interfere with the Stray, to our advantage, and a herdsman attended to the stock. According to a tombstone at Christ Church, William Hill, who died in 1868, was 'herdsman of Harrogate Stray for nearly forty years'.

The Stray had a lively aspect. In Edwardian days, a four-in-hand coach, complete with posthorn, plied for hire and the Stray was a place of entertainment, featuring a troupe of well-trained dogs, performing bears, German bands and Tom Coleman's pierrots. A night out in the town cost sixpence, which allowed for visiting a show (tuppence), a packet of cigarettes (one penny), a pint of beer (tuppence) and a fish and chip supper (one penny). Today, on Saturday evening, Harrogate is invaded by young people out for a good time at the many pubs, clubs and restaurants.

Harrogate is spacious, with broad tree-lined boulevards and an imposing array of Victorian buildings, some of them adorned by cast-iron canopies and floral arrangements. It proclaims itself to be a floral resort, which is astonishing considering its elevation and its exposure to all the winds that blow. In its heyday, palatial hotels were constructed, the number of bedrooms running into thousands. The green dome of the *Hotel Majestic* has the visual emphasis of an exclamation mark. The *Old Swan*, a splendid hotel, will forever be

8 & 9 Two contrasting views of West Park Stray. *Above*, a busy summer's day looking towards Burgess' Livery Stables, White Hart Mews. *Below*, looking down into Low Harrogate and, apart from the wandering cows, hardly a soul to be seen.

10 Montpellier Parade, West Park Stray in 1865.

11   The Harrogate Pierrots before the First World War.

associated with the sojourn of crime writer Agatha Christie, who had disappeared from her usual haunts in 1926 and whose whereabouts were of national concern. At the other end of the catering scale are public houses, none more interesting than *Hales Bar*, which has clung to its original features, such as gas lighting and cases of stuffed birds. Harrogate has cosy little tea-rooms where people gossip to the clink of delicate crockery. Bettys Tea Rooms, established in 1919, has for over thirty years now occupied a key position overlooking the gardens of Montpellier. Patrons sip their favourite brand of tea and consume home-made cakes and pastries while a pianist adds the magical touch of long-remembered airs.

At Harrogate, every open space—the Stray excepted—seems to have been planted up with flowers. The Harrogate I experienced forty years ago was beginning to assert a claim to be Britain's Floral Resort. In modern times, people still stroll rather than walk briskly through the Valley Gardens, the semi-wilderness where, on 'a fair summer's evening' in 1937, the author Edmund Vale observed rich folk dieting for their sins and men-servants and male nurses walking out respectable females of their own station. He saw miners taking rheumatic cures at one of the large institutions trying to escape from the embarrassing sight of opulent buildings. Nattily dressed servant girls, who had hastily cast aside cap and apron, were 'chaffing their local boys in a Tyneside accent, bound for the shady nooks of the pine-woods'. In early springtime, hard northern sunlight brings a responsive gleam from masses of crocuses and daffodils, which give way to beds of colourful tulips and, in summer, to a multi-coloured spectacle. Flowers deck the parks and numerous hanging baskets extend along the roadsides, form colourful displays on the traffic islands and stand to attention in well-ordered ranks at the Montpellier Gardens, a floriferous area in the town centre with a strong continental flavour.

A sense of freedom is felt during a walk through the Valley Gardens, a tract of land that had the prosaic name of Bogs Field, being the setting for many mineral wells. With the many wells now capped, the attention has switched to formal displays of plants, to trim lawns and to a sun pavilion with a stained-glass dome that was recently restored, partly with the support of Lottery money. A colonnade

12 & 13 *Right. The Old Swan* was built *c.*1700, but by 1878 it became the *Harrogate Hydro-pathic, below.*

14   The *Harrogate Hydropathic* in its old–time grandeur.

15   The *Hydropathic* reverted back to *The Old Swan* in 1952.

offers shade on summer days to any ladies who wished to keep their delicate complexion from the heat of the sun. Sulphur water obtained from the Royal Pump Room just allows a consumer to reach the Valley Gardens toilet block before taking effect. It is an easy walk from near the Old Pump Room to Harlow Car, sometimes rendered Harlow Carr, the footpath passing through resinous pinewoods and beside groves of rhododendrons to reach one of the North Country's most outstanding garden. It dates back to 1948, when Lt.-Col. Charles H. Grey, a descendant of the Hoares of Stourhead, who created outstanding 18th-century landscapes, presided over the Northern Horticultural Society. It was proposed, at a site on Crag Lane, to create 'a northern Wisley'. The organisers reckoned that if a plant grew well at Harlow Car it would be hardy enough for most parts of the north. Today, on 68 acres, the botanical and horticultural interest extends to rock gardens, vegetable and fruit plots. Here, too, is a museum of gardening, a shop and restaurant. Incidentally, Harlow Car's garden is in an area known in the 1840s as Harlow Car springs. Henry Wright, the landowner, cleaned

16 *Hales Bar* which retains its gas-lit Early Victorian interior.

17 Bettys Café was founded in 1919 by Frederick Belmont in this imposing Edwardian building that overlooks Montpellier Gardens.

out and protected one of the sulphurous springs and subsequently built a hotel and bath-house, arranging for spring water to be heated and charging half-a-crown to any visitor who wished to bathe. William Grainge, in his guide of 1861, called the hotel and the gardens that flanked it 'a sweet secluded spot'.

Harrogate's situation, to the east of the Pennines, means that it has a generally cheerful climate, being sunnier and drier than places just a few miles to the west. The Weather Clerk likes to surprise us. When Geoffrey Smith, a well-known broadcaster on gardening topics, started work as superintendent at Harlow Car in the winter of 1954-5, rain fell for three solid days, flooding the stream that divides the garden into two. 'Three of us had to wade waist-deep out of the machinery shed. The next morning, paths had washed out, spreading gravel on to the lawns. A bridge was carried away, taking with it most of the plants on the banks of the stream. In the boiler house, only the top door

18 & 19 Modern statuary and the Sun Pavilion in Valley Gardens.

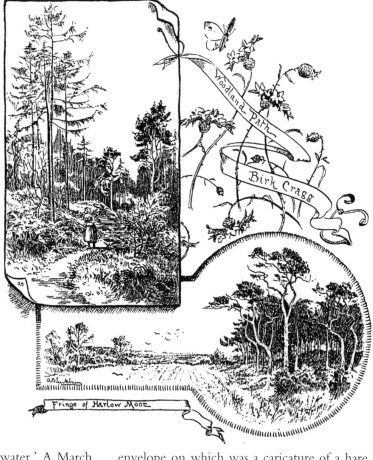

20 Fringe of Harlow Moor, a Victorian print from Edmund Bogg's *Eden Vale to the Plain of York*.

of the stove remained above water.' A March gale whipped out 20 trees, 'costing me at the same time a new tweed cap'.

In the West Riding's murky industrialised past, when mill chimneys belched forth smoke, Harrogate was free of airborne pollution. Henry Curling, writing early in the 19th century, set high-lying Harrogate on 'a bare Scotchified-looking common'. Bowden's *Directory* of 1895 referred to Harrogate as being 'situated upon lofty table land'. Lettice Cooper, the Yorkshire novelist, facing a Harrogate breeze, felt she was on top of the world. Arnold Kellett, who started his teaching career at Harrogate's Ashville College, knows of no English town of comparable size 'so open to invigorating moorland air'.

Forty years ago, I was amused to receive from the Corporation a letter in a brown envelope on which was a caricature of a hare, complete with suitcase, on which the name of the town was written. A slogan suggested that he might 'Hop over to Harrogate'. The idea of 'hopping' to this gracious Yorkshire town—this place described in a Victorian guide book as one of 'handsome stone-built parades, mansions, crescents and palatial hotels'—had not occurred to me. It would have been more appropriate to glide to Harrogate behind the softly-purring engine of a Rolls Royce or a Bentley or, perhaps, behind a high-stepping team of well-groomed horses. The Harrogate of my imaginings was a fashionable spa, the resort of fur-coated ladies and monocled, cigar-smoking men. Rightly or wrongly, I tended to think of Harrogate as a snobbish sort of place and also as a unique survival of late Victorian and Edwardian days. Lettice Cooper considered that, though the nearby wool towns of the West Riding bore the heavy stamp of Victoria, the spirit of Harrogate was Edwardian: 'It belongs to the days when it was fashionable to visit German spas. Then what is now the Royal Hall used to be called the Kursaal.' Miss Cooper found affinities, in some of the shops and the neatly-ordered beds of flowers, with a seaside resort such as Scarborough. Indeed, her Harrogate was 'the seaside without the sea'. Richard Muir, who was reared and now lives almost within sight of Harrogate, has referred to the town in its present state as embodying 'a strange blend of dowdy grandeur and yuppified vitality, the combination being made more wholesome by the retention of a Yorkshire grittiness and the keen climate from the upland winds which flurry and scurry across the Stray'.

I was soon aware, in compiling a history of the place, that Harrogate is dominated by its status as a spa. I was dealing with a huge cast, beginning with early tourists, doctors and their patients, hypochondriacs, the aristocrats who arrived in Harrogate in fine carriages to enjoy the events of the Season. Into the story come builders and councillors, hoteliers and shop-keepers, who in an astonishingly short time created a fine Victorian town. I pondered on

the Edwardian heyday of musical concerts and grand balls. When I drew some sulphur water from a tap beside the Pump Room, being already nauseated by the tang rising from a metal grate beneath my feet, I was conscious that Harrogate really began with a strong smell from the ground and that sulphur water was at the heart of the town's prosperity for several centuries. I had been warned, 'Don't smell it; just sup it!' I drew a measure of water, cupped my hands, and sipped the water, which not only stank but was flat, as well it might be, having taken such a time to rise from the depths of the earth. The effect of sulphur water on an over-laden human system can be dramatic, but was a local man joking who he told me that when a Liverpool football team had visited Harrogate, and the trainer told them to drink the sulphur water and then run through the Valley Gardens, he made a special point of telling them the location of the nearest public conveniences? It is said that when a grocer named Swan, who had a shop near the Old Sulphur Well, developed what was to become known as Farrah's toffee, he devised a pleasurable way of taking the nasty taste of sulphur from the mouths of those who had sampled the water.

21 Park Parade.

22   Interior of the Royal Hall, formerly the Kursaal.

23   Royal Parade before the First World War.

The first tourists belonged to the leisured classes who, inspired by the many guide books, set off to explore remoter parts of their native land. The spa-seekers were usually obese or ill. They hoped that by drinking or bathing in the mineral springs they would regain their health and vitality. The nastier the waters, the more benefit might be derived from them. None was nastier to the senses of taste and smell than sulphur water, which 'stinks noisomely, like rotten eggs', to quote the botanist Ray, who visited in 1661. By 1782, High Harrogate was stated to be 'one of the principal watering-places in the North of England, having eight very good inns, most of them large and spacious'. Like Matlock, the town was well-situated, with picturesque scenery close at hand. Early tourists were in love with the picturesque. The ivy-draped ruins of the old Cistercian abbey of Fountains, in the valley of the Skell, were particularly well regarded. The town reached its zenith in the first decade of the

19th century. By the second quarter of the century, spas in general were in decline. Already, people were questioning the claims regarding the medicinal benefits of the water and there had been a drift to seaside resorts, including the spa town of Scarborough. Harrogate's popularity was sustained by the strength and variety of the mineral springs, both here and at Starbeck, and by the pains it had taken to develop medical services.

The stamp of Victoria is immediately apparent in Harrogate, where her statue was given a prominent position and grand buildings and streets were associated with her by name. Yet Queen Victoria never set foot here. It was left to Princess Victoria, her grand-daughter, to inaugurate the royal association with the town. From a grand house, 11 York Place, she saw and doubtless enjoyed a view of the Stray, as did members of the Russian royal family and King Emmanuel of Portugal. Princess Alex, later Czarina to Nicholas II, stayed at Cathcart

24 Farrah's toffee shop in 1840.

House, West Park Stray. (Alex and other members of the family were murdered in the revolution of 1917.)

Harrogate is venerated by cyclists as the birthplace of the Cyclists' Touring Club, which is still in lusty existence. In 1885, when an article on bicycling appeared in the magazine of the Harrogate College, it was supposed that 'every horse is by this time accustomed to the sight of the machines', these being penny-farthings. 'The rage lately,' the writer of this article continues, 'has been for the so-called Safety bicycles, but their ugliness and the doubt as to whether the term Safety is not a misnomer has somewhat retarded their progress.' Incidentally, in 1894 the editor of the college magazine reported that the first county cricket match was played at Harrogate.

The Rev. Bernard Wray, who grew up at Harrogate in the 1920s, recalled for me when three of the springs, on assorted public buildings, were for the free use of the public. The iron water at St John's Well was drinkable, but the magnesia well in the Valley Gardens and the sulphur well on the Pump Room were not recommended as thirst quenchers. In 1939 when Ella Pontefract and Marie Hartley toured Yorkshire, Harrogate still retained a distinctive way of life. Ella mentioned Harrogate streets crowded with well-dressed people, and wrote of the dinners and cabaret shows being held at large hotels and the White Rose Players staging a popular play at the Opera House. While an orchestra played in the Valley Gardens on a summer afternoon, tea was served on the balcony of the café and, in dry weather, on the grass. Ella added: 'The brilliant colours of the flower-beds vie with the gay umbrellas and the dresses of the women; and there is an air of importance, as if lolling on camp chairs and sipping tea in these gardens were the only things worth doing on a sunny day.'

At the beginning of the Second World War, Harrogate was running down as a spa and many people were unemployed. Its Victorian and Edwardian heydays were long over, though

25   One of the grandest streets in Harrogate.

echoes of that glamorous period might be heard in the 1920s, when discerning visitors by rail patronised a horse-cab, one of a row of such outfits standing outside the station, or used the services of one of the hand-cart men in transporting the luggage. A large family contrived to hire one of each. Bath chairs, constructed using basketwork for lightness, and with protective covers in the event of rain, were available for public hire. Such a chair was pulled or steered by means of a long handle. If local people had continued to gear the economy to spa trade, the town would have become a musty showplace. War had been a blessing in disguise. The Town Clerk, J. Neville Knox, told me that in 1939 something like one-sixth of the houses on the Duchy of Lancaster estate were vacant, one of the best areas in town.

26   The former *Commercial* hotel (now *Cutlers on the Stray*) when it was the headquarters for the Bicycle Touring Club.

27   Members of Harrogate Cycling Club in the early 20th century.

28   The Magnesia Well in Valley Gardens, 1903.

29 Magnesia Well after it had been gutted by fire in August 1924.

30 A tea house in Valley Gardens.

31 Montpellier Hill and Cornwall Road in the 1880s. Notice the cabs awaiting hire beside Cornwall Road.

In 1953, ICI Fibres Division brought 1,500 top scientists to the town and spent about £3 million, which then was an appreciable sum, on buildings. Other large commercial concerns moved their administrative centres into town. Most of them have departed, yet Harrogate still has a busy aspect and the density of cars must be one of the highest in the land. Some of the town's grandeur went when central areas were infilled using modern styles of architecture. Pevsner, in his great work on the Buildings of England (1951-74), considered that the finest building in the spa was not a public building nor a church but the *White Hart* hotel.

In their later days as a medical centre, the Royal Baths were dealing almost exclusively with National Health Service patients so, in a sense, the celebrated mineral springs had been nationalised. To the town, in what are now days of yore, came sufferers from acute and chronic rheumatic diseases—from lumbago, sciatica, fibrositis, neuritis, rheumatoid arthritis, osteo-arthritis—as well as gout, obesity, skin diseases and nervous disorders. All that now remains of the old spa days is the Pump Room, now a museum, and the Turkish Baths, where a patron can take a shower or a bracing dip in the plunge pool, towel down and work a way through three inter-connecting hot room chambers and cool off by relaxing in the frigidarium—an experience not unlike that enjoyed by the Ancient Romans.

The Royal Hall, which was opened in 1903, and which becomes a centenarian in May 2003, is one of the architectural glories in need of attention. Its function changed 20 years ago with the opening of a new conference centre;

32 The *White Hart Hotel*, Low Harrogate, was built in 1846.

33   Satan passing over Harrogate Wells.

34 Harrowgate Wells in 1772. A hand-coloured engraving by Moses Griffiths.

henceforth, the Royal Hall was a place for entertainment and cultural activities. The Hall is awesome, having a 360-degree walkway around an auditorium with seating for 1,270 people. Conservation has a high price: when the Hall was re-roofed in 1990, the cost was £250,000, and £135,000 was spent on interior work in 1997-8 so that the building complied with fire regulations. But, if neglected, parts of the Hall might have to be closed. The fabric of the Royal Baths (a centenarian in 1997) shows signs of deterioration but expensive plans are in hand to renovate it.

Harrogate's good fortune was to become one of the earliest of many English spa towns. In the 17th century, when the medicinal properties of its mineral wells were first recognised, its waters were compared with those at Spa, in what is now Belgium, and during the subsequent spa-mania Harrogate vied with places like Bath, Buxton and Cheltenham. In marked contrast to ancient stonework are the radomes on Menwith Hill, west of Harrogate. They adorn the skyline like gigantic golf balls. Harrogate is also a shopping centre of great variety and quality. The town thrives on offices and light industry but, by and large, it has remained a place where people can walk with heads high and not scurry about, feeling like ants, as is the case in the centres of most large towns and cities. Harrogate Council built some tower blocks, to the dismay of the local people. Once there was a multitude of shops offering a diversity of goods and services and variety is still to be found but, as elsewhere, the chain stores have moved in and many people lament the dowdy look of some areas of the town that once were stylish. Harrogate is making an effort to revive something of the glamour of its days as a spa. The name Harrogate Spa has been bestowed on a locomotive and also a tulip. The Harrogate Civic Society, keen to remind residents and visitors of its glorious past as a spa, and with the interest and help of Harrogate Council, have reinstated two well-heads which, in the 18th century, covered the magnesia and chalybeate (iron) springs in the north-west corner of what are now the Valley Gardens. Harrogate, in its quest for modernity, has not forgotten the foundation of its fortunes.

Chapter Two

In the Beginning

The place-name Harrogate came into use early in the 14th century, with a mention in the roll of Knaresborough Court, where Bilton and Harrogate are 'hamlets' in the township of Killinghall. Other names used in the 14th century include Harugat, Harougat, Harowgat, Harowgate and Harwegate. The element *gate* is taken to mean 'a way'. Was the *gate* an access point for Harlow Hill? Or was it associated with Haverah, one of the old deer parks of the Forest of Knaresborough, a medieval concept that shaped local history from just after the Norman Conquest to the reign of George III? The second option was favoured by Edmund Bogg, a Victorian bookseller and scribe, who in his book *From Edenvale to the Plains of York* gives some romantic—indeed, fanciful—word pictures of Forest life. He asserted that a path or gate across the open forest to Haverah Park was 'the pathway to Heyrau, from which, by many slight alterations during the flight of time, we have received "the world-wide name of Harrogate".' Another use of *gate*, tinged by antiquity, was a right to pasture stock on the Stray, a prominent area of common land.

The Royal Forest of Knaresborough extended from the Nidd (north) to the Wharfe (south) and from Crimple Beck (east) to some way beyond the Washburn (west). At the north-western extremity stood Craven Cross, on Greenhow Hill, at an elevation of nearly 1,200 ft. Curiously, the forestland did not include Knaresborough, though the town was the venue of its chief court. This forest, like many another, was not an area of massed trees, as in the Hollywood version of Sherwood Forest, but a tract of land composed of moorland and wooded valleys. The root word *foris* implies waste ground kept for hunting and subject to Forest Law. Even this name is a misnomer, the Law being in truth a penal code, the breaking of which might lead to mutilation or death. Birds and beasts were protected from all but those empowered to hunt, so it was also an outstanding nature reserve.

In 1612, the unenclosed land amounted to over 45 square miles. Where Bilton Hall now stands was one of the enclosed deer parks, surrounded by paling that the tenants of Bilton had made using wood supplied by Forest officials. Bilton, Rosset, Killinghall, Scriven, Beckwith and Knaresborough had been mentioned in the Domesday Survey of 1086. Many early records concern disputes over land or produce, though the immediate neighbourhood of Harrogate was not valuable, being marshy, with streams flowing into numerous ponds and, elsewhere, heavy clay keeping the land chilled well into the springtime. As an example of a land dispute, it was alleged in 1347 that Adam de Roudon had carted marl from Robert Brown's land in Bilton, and a redress of one shilling was demanded by Brown. Petty quarrels were doubtless forgotten in the summer of 1349 when bubonic plague, which was to be known as the Black Death, in its remorseless sweep through Yorkshire,

35 Crossing the River Wharfe, by the Harrogate photographer Bertram Unne (1913–81).

36 Knaresborough from Castle Hill.

began to claim victims at nearby Knaresborough.

What became High Harrogate derived its importance as a meeting point of well-used ways, and by 1400 a chantry chapel had been established (to be dissolved in 1549; not for two centuries would Harrogate again have a church of its own). Small-time farmers drew their meagre income partly from land and livestock and partly from a variety of textile operations. The clack of the handloom might be heard mainly during inclement weather or at times of the year when farm work was slack. John Lindley of Harrogate left to his brother William in 1541 'a wollen loyme and all things perteyning thereunto'. William Lightfoot of Harrogate died in 1606 leaving, among other objects, 'a wooden loom with four pairs of woollen gears, one pair for harden [cloth woven from hempen yarn], and two pairs for linen thereto belonging'. William also left two spinning wheels, cards and combs. Both hemp and flax were grown locally. If a grower did not possess a loom, he might arrange with a poor cottager to weave it for him. From some of this varied textile activity arose the celebrated Knaresborough linen industry.

In the 16th century, with the rising demand for land, there was talk of splitting up the Forest among individual owners. This eventually occurred, with Parliamentary authority, in 1770, the first Act causing all the 'wastes' of the Forest to be divided, and much land being assigned to the Duchy of Lancaster. The Forest Award of 1778 excepted the 215-acre Stray, which became public property, certain local inhabitants having rights of pasturage and everybody guaranteed access to the mineral wells which, by this time, were being well patronised. The Tewit Well, the first to become popular, must have been known (if only for its noxious taste) since earliest times, yet the Harrogate story might be said to begin with the romantic tale of its discovery in 1571 by William Slingsby (1525/7-1606), a nephew of Sir William Slingsby and a member of a family renowned in Yorkshire. William, who lived at nearby Bilton Hall, had sampled mineral waters when visiting Spa in Belgium and he was aware of their medicinal use. Now, by equating Spa with the Tewit Well, and telling a medical friend about it, he initiated a process that would eventually lead to Harrogate becoming one of the most notable spa towns in England.

Chapter Three

The Early Spa

The Slingsby story is first mentioned in print by Dr. Edmund Deane (1572-1615). This York physician had a healthy interest in the history of the mineral wells. He could find no one earlier than Slingsby who had recognised the medicinal value of the Tewit Well. Slingsby had the Well paved and walled, as much for his own benefit as for others. He visited it regularly and declared that it excelled 'the tart fountaines beyond the seas' and was 'more quick and lively and fuller of minerall spirits'. To the Tewit Well, and to others that were discovered within a radius of a mile or two, came a motley company of invalids, hypochondriacs and medical folk.

In 1596, some twenty years after Slingsby's experience, Dr. Timothy Bright (1551-1615), a physician and subsequently rector of Barwick-in-Elmet, who was also a friend of Deane, dubbed the area 'the English Spaw' and advised others to use it. Deane recorded that Bright 'did not onely direct and advise others to it, but himselfe … would use it in the Sommer season'. The 'English Spaw' was the 'Glory of Knaresborough' and most of those who visited it used Knaresborough as a base in preference to lodging at one of the well-scattered farms. Indeed, according to research by Dr. Arnold Kellett, medical men throughout the 17th century, when debating the merits of various watering-places, always referred to this as the Knaresborough Spa. Standing at the edge of a deep gorge carved by the Nidd, the 'shining river' of the Celtic folk, Knaresborough

was a long-established community, with a castle and parish church as focal points. The town had a market that thrived in an especially large market place and, of special relevance to those planning to take the waters, there were inns. When, in 1626, Edmund Deane's observations were published as *Spadacrene Anglica*, or *The English Spaw Fountaine*, the five springs that were identified included the Dropping Well at Knaresborough, St Mungo's at Copgrove and

37 Knaresborough's Dropping Well.

38 St Robert's Chapel and Castle Montague, Knaresborough.

39 Knaresborough Castle.

40 Spawing at Harrogate, Harry Garrett, 1906.

St Robert's near Knaresborough, where the water was 'pure and simple', a fact unrecognised by the poor and ignorant, who drank copious quantities in the hope of miracle cures.

At Harrogate, Deane described four springs, three of which yielded sulphur water. One well lay in Bilton Park and another, 'near unto the towne', became known as Starbeck Old Spa. The English Spaw Fountaine, which was a powerful spring 'beyond a place called Hargate Head in a bottom on the right hand of it, as you goe and almost in the side of a little brook', became known as the Old Sulphur Well—locally 'the Stinking Spaw'—the water being noted for its purgative action. The wells of Harrogate, as enthusiastically promoted by doctors, could cure virtually every known ailment. Deane considered that the Tewit Well (also known as Common Spring) was good for cleansing the internal organs. Sufferers from the dropsy, jaundice, dizziness, epilepsy and drying the moist brain might bear it in mind. Children were not overlooked; the mineral waters combated worms and distemper. Ladies with 'the green sickness' would benefit. It was recommended that sufferers should visit Harrogate between late June and mid-September, when the air was at its purest, hottest, cleanest and driest.

Michael Stanhope, yet another friend of Deane, provided a description of the mineral springs in 1626, the year in which Deane's book was published. Stanhope's work, *Newes out of Yorkshire*, bore a cumbersome subtitle: 'An account of the true discovery of a soveraigne Minerall, Medicinall Water, in the West Riding of Yorkshire, neere an ancient Towne called Knaresborough, not inferior to the Spa in Germany.' (It was actually in Belgium.) In 1631, Stanhope chanced upon what became known as the Sweet Spaw, reporting in his book *Cures without Care* (1632) that it lay on firm ground, as compared with the marshy conditions around the Tewit Well. (The Sweet Spaw is known today as St John's Well, having taken its name not from the evangelist but from one John Hardestie, an attendant here during the 19th century. John was a good advertisement for the waters; he lived to the age of ninety-six.)

Stanhope's writings lauded the properties of the chalybeate springs of High Harrogate and also the sulphur springs of Low Harrogate. He noted that one spring (the Old Sulphur Well) had 'beene long knowne by the name of the stinking well'. A York shoemaker who suffered so badly from scurvy that he feared for his life, drank the sulphur water at home, in the middle of winter, and was cured within a month. 'There is nothing more common than for people to frequent this sulphur well and get cured of their ulcers and sores by washing in it.' Stanhope's wealthy patients were upset by the insanitary ways of their social inferiors, some of whom left dirty bandages and even 'wash their soares and cleanse their besmeared clouts (though unseene) where divers after dippe their cups to drinke'. By taking the waters at the Sweet Spaw, the Countess of Buckingham was cured of asthma. Accommodation being limited to rooms in a few cottages and farmsteads, which did not suit the Countess, she lived in a tent pitched near the well. Perhaps her asthma benefited from the fresh air rather than the water. Nevertheless, accounts of near-miraculous cures were circulating far and wide: a distinguished lady from York was relieved of terrible swellings after the birth of her children; another enjoyed relief from dreadful headaches.

By now, the Civil War was raging, but it had little direct impact on Harrogate, though a decisive battle was fought in July 1644 on Marston Moor, which lay between Harrogate and York. The Royalists were soundly defeated and the Parliamentarians moved on to surround Knaresborough Castle in the autumn of that year. Lord Morley, who was ensconced there because he had been taken by surprise when the troops appeared, wrote to Lord Fairfax, the Parliamentary commander, requesting safe conduct for himself and four servants. The 'vacillation of these distracted and ruinous times' meant that Deane's book had been 'almost lost and obliterated'. Deane died in 1640 and nine years later a new edition of the book was issued by a York chemist called John Taylor, who praised the mineral springs, noting that an ailing person who sipped the water would find it benefited 'the liver, splen, kidneis, and other interiour parts'. It also 'clenseth and purifieth the whole masse of blood contained in the veynes by purging it from cholericke, phlegmaticke and melancholicke humours … migrims, turnings, swimmings of the head and

braine … It cheereth and reviveth the spirits, strengtheneth the stomacke, causeth a good and quicke appetite.'

By the middle of the 17th century, visitors to the Harrogate area were bathing in heated sulphur water and accommodation for visitors had marginally improved. Anyone staying at a farmhouse was at least assured of fresh produce to eat. Some farms became the hotels of later years. When George Neale, a doctor of Leeds, wrote *Spadacrene Eboracensis*, his incomplete treatise being incorporated in Short's *History of Mineral Waters* (1734), there were over twenty bathing houses (lodgings with tubs) in Low Harrogate. With no piped water available, the bather depended on water-women for a supply of mineral water.

The bathing routine was to be a feature of Harrogate life for many years. In winter, some local entrepreneurs boiled mineralised water and sent the salt to customers in London, though they already had the benefits of Epsom Salts, extracted from the spa waters of the capital. Dr. Short denounced 'mad frolics', adding, 'Luxury, intemperance, unseasonable hours, idleness, gratification of taste and appetite are become so fashionable.' The state of a local house [inn] when Lady Verney descended on Harrogate in 1665 was summed up as being 'horidly nasty, and crowded up with all sorte of company … and it sure hathe nethor been well cleaned nor ared this dousen years …'. John French, 'Doctor of Physick', wrote and published *The Yorkshire Spaw* in 1652 and gave us the first good description of 'Bogs Field', about 240 yards above the head of the Old Sulphur Well, where most of the springs were to be found. The bog had a diameter of about twenty yards and 'in the said bog I found three or four sorts of waters, viz. A Sulphur, and Vitriolene, and of each two sorts'. French, who was about to leave the area, thought that, if someone spent some time and money in digging up the bog 'and erecting some Wels there', it was possible that a new and better spring might be found.

41   Old Sulphur Well and Bog Gardens.

Initially, no charge was made for spa water, though inevitably local people cashed in to the extent of serving water on the spot or transporting it to local lodgings. Dr. George Neale, of Leeds, was surely over-dosing his patients in 1656 when he urged them to drink three or four pints at a time of water drawn from the Old Sulphur Well, in Low Harrogate, and asserting that if that did not have any effect, they might try one or two more pints. Sufferers from rheumatism, gout and skin diseases were said to have their troubles alleviated by bathing in spa water from which the chill had been taken.

'The Spaws of Knaresborough' were glimpsed by the diarist John Evelyn when he climbed the central tower of York Minster in 1654 and, when the monarchy had been re-established under Charles II in 1660, Harrogate spa began a period of steady expansion. The waters were being used for drinking or for bathing, and the town found its qualities as a spa being compared with Scarborough. Dr. George Tonstall, who had proclaimed the superior qualities of Scarborough, had a change of heart—and so had his patients—when he was persuaded that 'Knaresborough Spa' had the superior virtues. John Ray, the naturalist, took time off from plant-hunting in 1661 to visit the wells and at St Mungo's Well saw a 'great number of poor people'. They 'put on their shirts wetted in the water, letting them dry upon their backs.' (St Mungo's was being recommended to sufferers of weak limbs and rickets.) Ray and his companion next visited the Spaw at Harrogate and drank of the water, noting, 'It is not unpleasant to the taste, somewhat acid and vitriolock. Then we visited the sulphur well, whose water, though it be pellucid enough, yet stinks noisomely like rotten eggs or sulphur auratum diaphoreticum.' Marmaduke Rawdon of York, who called at the Old Sulphur Well in 1664, observed that it 'stinks like the smell of a sinke or rotten eggs, but is very medicinable for many diseases ...'. Ralph Thoresby, the Leeds antiquary, travelled to Harrogate on 14 June 1681. Here he lived with cousins, enjoying 'much company to the Spaws ... Drank the sulphur water plentifully.' Thoresby was back later in the month and twice in July, drinking the waters.

Knaresborough was still favoured as a base by the discriminating, among whom might be numbered an intrepid woman traveller, Celia Fiennes, who rode side-saddle through the land, looking for mineral waters. She found lodgings at Knaresborough in 1697, some sixty years after a visitor season had become established. Considering her interest in spas, Celia probably had with her a copy of Deane's book, the third edition of which was published in 1654. If so, she would have read of the supposed link between the sulphur springs and the mines and brimstone beneath the ground; also that the water from these springs turned silver into a copper hue. Three springs were mentioned. Water drawn at the Sulpher (*sic*) or 'Stinking Spaw', alias the Old Sulphur Well, was clear in appearance but produced a white scum. The smell was strong and offensive and Celia likened it to carrion or a jakes (latrine). She was put out when her steed refused to go near the spot because of the stench. Celia drank a quart each morning for two days and considered it 'a good sort of Purge if you can hold your breath so as to drink them down'. At the 'Sweet Spaw' or 'Chalibiet' spring, which was later known as St John's chalybeate, the water was noted for its iron content and she found here a basin within an arched stone cover. Third was the 'Common' water spring, almost certainly the Tewit Well, which she considered was good for bathing the eyes and for drinking purposes.

Chapter Four

Georgian Elegance

The spa villages of High and Low Harrogate became celebrated through the testimony of medical folk and also by means of the printed word. Books began to pour from the flatbed presses of the printers. At a straggle of buildings along the edge of the common, the well-to-do encountered the 'indigenous poore' who were 'plain husbandmen and cottagers'. The experience of 'taking the waters' in poor weather was rigorous, there being little available cover and no toilet facilities. Stanhope noted, 'What unseemly shifts have I seen many strangers of note put to for want of a convenient place of retirement.' This they most certainly needed when they had imbibed 'frequent draughts of this water, which is apt (with some violence) now and then to open the body'. The wells being set on 'a rude barren Moore … those that are weake … receive more prejudice by the piercing bleake aire, than benefit by the water'. At the Old Sulphur Well in Low Harrogate, folk scattered their 'putrid rags' up and down. Stanhope's solution was to find 'within a quarter of a mile' one or two wells 'of the same equall worth which may be appropriated for the meaner sort'. In 1694, the Overseers of Pannal parish arranged for Dorothy Scarr, a pauper who was sick, to visit the Sulphur Well for treatment. She was lodged overnight at the house owned by Widow Hardisty, who received 3s. for providing Dorothy with '2 bathes'.

Quarrels broke out as people clamoured to take the waters. In 1675 the Constable, one Henry Bentley, recorded in his accounts relating to Low Harrogate an outlay of tenpence 'ffor going twice to Sulphur Well to cease quarrells'. Dr. John French was concerned that his patients might put on too much weight and warned that 'this water for the most part begetteth a very great appetite, by reason whereof many forget themselves at Table, putting in more than nature can dispose of.' In the 1660s, 'several slow Springs' noticed in the Bog Field by Dr. Simpson were excavated further. A spring on the north side of the field, provided with a stone basin, became known (inaccurately) as the Alum Well. A bathing-tub was a prized possession. The inventory of John Canlove, dated 18 December 1692, recorded that a bathing-tub and a bedstead were to be found in his west parlour. About the year 1663, Dr. George Neale, of Leeds, opened a bathing house beside the Sweet Spa in High Harrogate: patrons could bathe in sulphur water from which the natural chill had been taken. Neale popularised the practice to the extent that his type of sulphur bath came into use in spa towns overseas. His treatise on Low Harrogate mentioned that each bathing house situated near the Old Sulphur Well had the necessary conveniences; all were in full use during the Season. Bathing in hot, mineral-rich water was widely recommended by doctors to ease the pains of rheumatism, sciatica and gout.

A distinction was made between the lodging house and a bathing house. The lodging house proprietors offered food as well as accommodation, whereas 'bathing houses' were just that. The routine adopted by wealthier folk was bathing in the evening, followed by profuse sweating under heavy (not always clean) blankets, and a return to the lodging house in the hope of sleep. In Low Harrogate, the demand for such treatment led to the illegal appearance of a rash of new buildings on the common land beside the Old Sulphur Well. The Honour Court tried to combat it by levying fines, but these became standardised and were made with such regularity they were equated with paying rent. Dr. John Neale of Doncaster—the son of the aforementioned George Neale—recorded his use of 'a very cold Well at Harrogate, famed for sore Eyes'. He turned this well into a Cold Bath, 'with very good Conveniences and Accommodations for Strangers'. Lady Elmes, visiting 'the nasty Spaw' on a June day in 1665, 'began to drinke the horid sulfer watter, which all thowgh as bad as is posable to be immajaned, yet in my judgment plesant, to all the doings we have within doorse'. Her lodging was a 'horidly nasty' house, 'crowded up with all sorte of company, which we Eate with in a roome as the spiders are redy to drope into my mouthe, and sure hath nethor been well cleaned nor ared this doseuen yerese, it makes me much moare sicke than the nasty water …'

As accommodation was provided at Harrogate, those who had offered such facilities at Knaresborough saw their clientele whittled down. Harrogate's first recorded inn, which became known as the *Queen's Head*, was built in 1687 on a site half-way between the two major wells of High Harrogate. Several years later came the *Sinking Ship*, subsequently known as *The Granby*. The Leeds antiquary, Ralph Thoresby, writing at the turn of the century,

42 *The Granby*, named after the Marquis of Granby who fought in the Seven Years' War. Blind Jack used to play the fiddle here.

43 A Victorian engraving of *The Granby*.

was astonished at the way the place had grown in not much more than a decade, spreading from around the Tewit Well in High Harrogate to the sulphur wells that had been found in Low Harrogate. This area would not assume a tidy and respectable appearance for many years. Some gory sights were to be seen among the seriously ill who were taking the cure. Abraham de la Pryme, antiquary, recorded in 1695 how an ailing lad who had been vomiting blood was 'made to drink heartily of the water' and 'vomitted up a skin, something like a bladder, full of clotted blood'. Hopefully, the lad—and any spectators—made a quick recovery.

In about 1695, *The Crown* and *White Hart* hotels were opened in Low Harrogate, the former standing immediately opposite the Old Sulphur Well and, most likely, being an extension of an existing building. Also handy to the Well was *The Crescent*. The shape of the spa villages was determined by the inns and their relation to the most popular wells. At Low Harrogate, *The Crown* stood immediately opposite the Old Sulphur Well and, at the turn of the century, Jonathan Sutt began to receive visitors at 'The Sign of The Swan' (*Old Swan Hotel*). The Harrogate Season, which brought many well-to-do folk into town, opened in May, waxed in high summer and waned in September. Thomas Amory, author of *The Life and Opinions of John Buncle, Esquire*, about a man who visited the town in 1731, left us some striking pen pictures of the social life, which was marked by 'a certain rural plainness and freedom mixed, which are vastly pleasing'. At Harrogate were to be found 'gentlemen of the country and women of birth and fortune', including Sir Walter Calverley of Esholt, a business visitor to Knaresborough in 1699 who then moved on to 'the spaws at Harrowgate' for a ten-day visit, with another day spent at Leeds Quarter Sessions. It was a period when, according to a Dr. Short, the place was 'no longer the Hospital of Invalids but too often the Rendezvous of Wantonness and, not seldom, of mad Frolicks'. Those who found relief were people 'of mean Circumstances'; the rich indulged themselves. 'Luxury, taste and Appetite are become so fashionable.'

44 Montpellier Road at its junction with Crescent Road, *c.*1835. The most prominent building was a pump house built over a mineral well. The area round about was developed as a pleasure garden for the *Crown Hotel.*

45 *The Crown* was built in 1740 by Joseph Thackwray, rebuilt in 1847, and added to in 1870.

In any case, the influx of fashionable society led to price rises that the ordinary people could not afford.

A community without a church was unthinkable. Lady Elizabeth Hastings, one of the regular visitors, gave £50 for a church-building fund that was opened in 1743. Land for a new church, situated on the common, was given by the proprietors of *The Crown*. St John's Chapel opened its doors in 1749 to 'the Glory of God and the good of Mankind more Especially of the Inhabitants of Harrowgate with Bilton ... and such as thither Resort for the use of the Minerall Waters ...'

For years, roads were maintained by householders. Each had a statutory obligation to give three days of free labour annually to the task. As what was to become known as the Industrial Revolution got under way, and the necessity to have better roads for the movement of raw materials and manufactured goods arose, turnpike roads, to be maintained by tolls collected at roadside bars, were authorised by Parliament. Between 1753 and 1777 three such roads affected the township of Bilton-with-Harrogate: these were the road leading west from High Harrogate to Skipton, the turnpike to Leeds, and that running north-eastwards to Knaresborough and Boroughbridge. Harrogate being affected by three roads, a legal appeal was made and judgement given at a Special Sessions held at Knaresborough in 1786. The township was freed from the legal obligation of three days' labour for maintenance, on the Leeds turnpike, and had the work demanded for the Knaresborough and Boroughbridge road reduced to a single day.

Much of the roadwork was carried out under the supervision of a remarkable local man, John Metcalf of Knaresborough, subsequently known as Blind Jack, whose ideas began the era of scientific road-making. He was born in 1717 and though his parents were relatively poor they sent him to school at the age of four. He lost his sight as a consequence of smallpox. At his mother's insistence, he was taught how to play the fiddle and soon John Metcalf, the blind fiddler-boy from Knaresborough, was being employed by hoteliers at Harrogate. He was a popular figure in the Long Room of the *Queen's Head*. His road-making followed the introduction of an Act for the Boroughbridge turnpike, which covered a distance of about twelve miles. The planning and road construction was undertaken by a surveyor named Ostler, a friend of Metcalf. Metcalf persuaded the surveyor to let him undertake a three-mile section and supervised every aspect of the work, walking six miles daily to be on site by 6 a.m. In this way he was able to assess the type of ground the road would cross. He completed the three-mile length between Minskip and Ferrensby on time and to the satisfaction of the surveyor. Jack's next road-making project lay between Knaresborough and Harrogate. He resumed his practice of walking slowly and deliberately over the whole length. A big man, weighing 17 stone, he strode along carrying a great staff.

46 John Metcalf, better known as Blind Jack of Knaresborough.

47 & 48 *Queen's Hotel*, which may date from as early as 1660 was originally called the *Queen's Head*. The present building dates from 1855.

49 *Cedar Court Hotel*, formerly the *Queen's Hotel*.

Blind Jack put into practice a revolutionary method of making the foundations of a road in marshy conditions. He arranged for whin (gorse) and ling (heather) to be cut and formed into tight bundles. These were laid on soft ground to consolidate it. So pleased were the authorities when this road was completed in time that Metcalf was paid well, fee and bonus amounting to the not inconsiderable sum of £400. Next, he was invited to build a six-mile road between Harrogate and Harewood Bridge, to the south of the town, much of the route being on clayey ground in the former Forest of Knaresborough. He cleared the tough and tangled vegetation by harnessing nine draught-horses to a huge wheel-plough and setting them to work dragging it through the undergrowth. Onto the course of the road went durable layers of gravel and stone so that well before winter—the agreed completion time—the new road was available to the travelling public. Jack Metcalf was paid £1,200 for this work. By 1792, Blind Jack of Knaresborough had constructed 180 miles of turnpike. Tolls were charged in order to maintain the roads. On the Skipton turnpike, for example, tollbars were situated near the junction with Bilton Lane, at Grimbald Bridge and Flaxby, and at Harewood, Buttersyke and Killinghall. In 1752, it cost 9d. to travel in a two-horse conveyance between Harrogate and Leeds, a price that had risen to 1s. 3d. by the 1790s. Heavy carts were used to transport coal to Harrogate, this being needed to heat water at the sulphur baths as well as domestically, and a preferential rate was in force, that of 1752 for a four-horse wagon loaded with coal or lime being 4d.

A flurry of leaflets written by doctors and extolling the virtues of the spa waters included one produced by a Dr. French in 1760. He advised those with weak stomachs first to warm the waters and also to take exercise. 'In more particular, I forbid all flesh that is very salt, and fat, as bacon, pork, neats feet, tripes, ducks, geese, gizards of poultry, all salt fish, eels … I disapprove not of beef if it has been salted but

a week, especially for those who love it.' In the 1760s, Mrs. Wilks, who owned *The Granby*, converted a barn attached to Granby Farm into a theatre and charged a swingeing 2s. for admission. The plays had suggestive titles. There was one called *Clandestine Marriage* and a farce entitled *The Virgin Unmasked, or an old man taught wisdom*. The theatre was switched to new, more commodious premises on the east side of Church Square in 1788, the cost being met by the benevolent Mrs. Wilks. Tate Wilkinson's company of players visited Harrogate, and Samuel Butler's 'circuit troop' came to town, giving three shows a week during the high season, from 10 July until 22 September. The show began at 6.30 p.m. and took in two short plays with a vocalist performing during an interval. Butler, who recognised the publicity value of name-dropping, would adorn the poster for a particular play with the name of a distinguished patron who had 'desired' that the play should be presented. On one occasion it was the Most Noble the Marquis of Ely. Another production was staged 'by particular desire' of Lady Massey.

One account of a visit to Harrogate in 1763 was left by the Rev. Dr. Alexander Carlisle, Church of Scotland minister and bachelor living at Inveresk. In July, he set out on a holiday with a Dr. Wright, a professor at Glasgow University. They stayed at *The Dragon*, a house not only frequented by the Scots but 'the favourite home of the English nobility and gentry'. A general observation was that Harrogate was very pleasant, having 'a constant succession of good company and the best entertainment of any watering place in Britain at the least expense'. At breakfast-time they paid only tuppence each for muffins as it was the fashion for the ladies to furnish tea and sugar. Dinner was a shilling and supper sixpence. Wine and other extras were 'at the usual price and as little as you please; horses and servants at a reasonable rate. We had two haunches of venison twice a week. The ladies gave afternoon tea and coffee in their turns

50 A caricature of 'Taking the Cure'.

51 The *Dragon Hotel* from an engraving of 1852.

which, coming but once in four or five weeks, amounted to a trifle.' The visitors found that Harrogate

> abounded with half-pay officers and clergymen. The first are much the same at all times—ill educated but well-bred. Of the clergy, I have never seen so many together before and I [a Presbyterian minister] was able to form of a true judgement of them. They are in general— I mean the lower order—divided into bucks and prigs; of which the first, though inconceivably ignorant and sometimes indecent in their morals, yet I held them to be the most tolerable because they were unassuming and had no other affection but that of behaving themselves like gentlemen.

What of the gentlemen? This was the first time Carlisle had seen John Bull at any of his watering-places. He concluded that 'John' was an honest and worthy person but was seldom happy at home. At his watering places, free from domestic shackles, however, his reserve was overcome by the frankness of those he met. 'The man of £10,000 per annum can spend no more than the man of £500, so that the honest man finds himself quite unfettered and is ready to show his kind and sociable disposition and what he really is—the very best sort of man in the world.'

Tobias Smollett, the novelist, visited Harrogate in May 1766. His novel *Humphry Clinker* gives us an account of his experiences of the hot-bath-and-sweat routine that for many years was inflicted on gullible visitors to Harrogate:

> At night I was conducted into a dark hole on the ground floor, where the tub smoked and stunk like the pot of Acheron in one corner, and in another stood a dirty bed provided with thick blankets, in which I was to seat after coming out of the bath. My heart seemed to die within me when I entered this dismal bagnio and found my brain assaulted by such insufferable effluvia ... Being ashamed to recoil upon the threshold, I submitted to the process.

Our hero was in the tub for over a quarter of an hour. Then he was switched to the bed and lay swaddled in blankets for 'a full hour, panting with intolerable heat, but not the least moisture appearing upon my skin. I was carried to my chamber and passed the night without closing an eye in such a flutter of spirits as rendered me the most miserable wretch in being.' He had 'a violent hemorrhage' and 'lost two pounds of blood and more'. He became weak and languid 'but, I believe, a little exercise will forward my recovery'.

In Smollett's time, the accommodation at the Harrogate inns was strained. 'One of the Inns is already full up to the very garretts, having no less than fifty lodgers, and as many servants.' The water was repulsive.

> It is said to have effected so many surprising cures. I have drank [*sic*] it once, and the first draft has cured me of all desire to repeat the medicine. Some people say it smells of rotten eggs, and others compare it to the scourings of a foul gun ... I was obliged to hold my nose with one hand while I advanced the glass to my mouth with the other; and after I had made shift to swallow it, my stomach could hardly retain what it had received. The only effects it produced were sickness, griping and insurmountable disgust. I can hardly mention it without puking.

In 1769, the major topic at Harrogate was the proposed enclosure of the Royal Forest of Knaresborough. As a consequence of local representation to Parliament, commissioners were appointed to survey the area of the mineral springs, with which the future of the burgeoning community was bound up. In the following year, an Act of Parliament secured for public use that part of the Forest of Knaresborough associated with the Wells and popularly known as The Stray, seemingly because livestock strayed there freely for pasture. The Act declared that

> the said two hundred acres of land shall for ever hereafter remain open and uninclosed; and all persons whomsoever shall and may have free access at all times to the said springs, and be at liberty to use and drink the waters there arising and take the benefit thereof ... without

being subject to the payment of any acknowledgement whatever for the same or liable to any action of trespass or other suit, molestation or disturbance whatsoever in respect thereof.

Mining or quarrying that might damage the mineral springs would not be permitted.

The enclosure award was made in 1778. High and Low Harrogate were now forever bonded together by a crescent of open ground. Large areas of land in Harrogate were allocated to notable families, including the Ingilbys of Ripley and the Thackwrays. *The Crown* retained much of the old Forest by right of the Duchy of Lancaster. Rights of pasturage on the Stray were assigned to 27 private individuals, most of whom had already done well out of the enclosure of common land. The term relating to pasturage was 'gate', a single gate equating with one cow, a two-year-old horse or four sheep, and, in the allocation of gates, the Ingilbys of Ripley had a major share. (Such gates might be sold and, indeed, by 1836, they were held by only eight of the original owners of such rights; the others had been bought out by incomers.)

The Award of 1778 gave the assurance that two drinking places would be available to the people in perpetuity. One source of water, in High Harrogate, was at a place 'near the World's End Inn' (Grove House). The other, in Low Harrogate, was variously known as Cold Well, Bath or Spring. Water from this source was so popular with those staying at *The Crown* it was placed on the tables in black bottles. There was still much to be done to make conditions tolerable, however. Footways rather than roads connected the two spa villages, and these were dusty in summer, muddy in winter. This prompted Horace Walpole to declare in 1790, 'One would think the English were ducks. They are for ever waddling to the waters.' According to Ely Hargrove, of Knaresborough (writing in 1782),

> such numbers of the nobility and gentry have annually resorted here [since 1740] that it has become one of the principal watering places in the North of England, having eight very good inns, most of them large and spacious … The inns being at some distance from each other, their respective lodgers form distinct societies and live in the most social and agreeable manner.

They invariably drank the waters before breakfast, some of them being driven to the wells in carriages. They spent much of what remained of the day on excursions into the surrounding district. If the weather was inclement, the denizens of the big hotels played cards or billiards

52   A coach and four preparing to set off from the Stray, 1911.

or read books and papers from a circulating library. The shops of Harrogate were attractive to the ladies. Hargrove noted that public balls were held each Monday and Friday 'at each house in rotation'. Popularity had its price. Pressure on the few footpaths across the Stray could lead to frayed nerves, such as when two sedan chairs were in collision as the bearers sought to maintain a course on the driest part of a muddy path. A brawl occurred, urged on by the wealthy folk within, one of whom fell into the mud.

Bystanders at the Harrogate Theatre would be astonished by the sight of the well-to-do arriving in their fine carriages, among whom was Alexander Wedderburn, Lord Loughborough, who now had a local home, Wedderburn House, completed in the Adam style in 1786. When attending the theatre in his smart horse-drawn carriage, his lordship used a relatively short and smooth ride across The Stray. He had been a patron of the local theatre since one was first established in 1785, making it possible for talented stage performers to become recognised. Among those who performed at Harrogate was an actress with the unforgettable name of Tryphosa Jane Wallis. Each Wednesday a 'fish machine' travelled from Stockton to Leeds by way of Harrogate and left supplies of the choicest fish at the big hotels. A shortage of fish was the subject of comment in one of the plays presented by Mr. Butler's company. On 6 July 1790, theatre-goers were amused during the staging of Farquhar's Restoration comedy, *The Beaux Strategem*, when the landlord Bonniface observed: 'As for fish, truly Sir, we are an inland town and indifferently provided with fish, that's the truth on't.'

As the years went by, the popularity of the spa was maintained but treatments changed and the recommended consumption of sulphur water declined from three or four to two pints a day. A bather still had to endure relatively long inundation in water 'as hot as it is well bearable', the session ending when the attendant felt the 'constitution' of the patient would

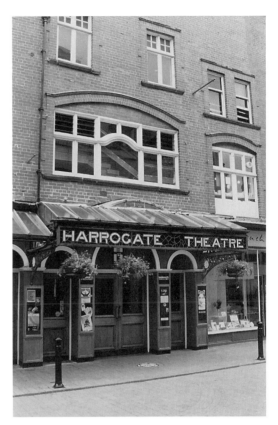

53 Harrogate Theatre which was built in 1900 as the Grand Opera House.

bear no more. By 1792, Harrogate had dispensed, too, with the notion of 'the common seating bed'. When used successively by many people, it had been distinctly unhygienic. By 1786, when the St John Well was distinguished by a lofty dome, the expense was met by the aforementioned Lord Loughborough (Alexander Wedderburn). In the grand hotels of High Harrogate—in *The Queen, Granby* and *Dragon*—the 'cream' of society gathered during the season. The attention of the medical fraternity and their patients had switched mainly to the wells of Low Harrogate. The Old Sulphur Well now vied for attention with a group of wells, of various kinds, from the Crescent Water (chloride of iron) to St George's Spaw (chalybeate, which contained iron).

Hargrove, writing in 1789, mentioned that buildings of all descriptions increased every year 'and several of the inns now receive annually more company than the whole town had held forty years before. The company was sociable, the air 'lively, bracing, exhilarating' and the district offered 'pleasing and delightful scenes'. Henry Skrine was similarly impressed with Harrogate, observing, 'To do justice to it I must declare a fortnight may be spent here with as much novelty and pleasure … as any Publick Place in England.'

In 1793, the spirit of The Stray was violated by Colonel Clement Wolsley, who laid out a racecourse that was 16 yards wide and a mile-and-a-half in circumference. It was not used much and nothing remains of this sporting enterprise except the wistful memories of those such as Henry Curling, who wrote, 'If the running was not quite so good as at Newmarket or Doncaster, the fun was greater.' The attendance was 'genteel' and the equipages on the course were 'elegant'. Between and after the races, rural sports were to be seen. One involved 'chasing pigs with soaped tailes'. Races took place between 'strapping wenches' with a chemisette as a prize. 'Rough-headed louts' clambered up a greasy pole for a leg of mutton lodged at the top.

As the century turned, the demand grew for a public assembly room, to be financed by public subscription. It was almost completed in May 1806, according to the *Leeds Mercury*, which noted that 'it will be opened on 16th June with some select pieces of music on the organ'. The Promenade Rooms (now the Mercer Gallery) formed an 'elegant and commanding building', situated in a garden and intended as a 'morning lounge' for those who assembled every morning at the wells. Among the celebrities who lectured here were Oscar Wilde, reporting on his visit to the United States, and Stanley, relating the details of his encounter with Dr. Livingstone in Central Africa. A lady who wrote *A Season in Harrogate* (1811) recalled the bathing in verse:

Astonished I saw when I came to my doffing,
A tub of hot water made just like a coffin,
In which the good woman who attended the bath,
Declar'd I must lie down as straight as a lath,
Just keeping my face above water, that so
I might better inhale the fine fumes from below …

By 1818, there were nine hotels and inns: *The Granby*, *Dragon*, *Queen's Head*, *Hope Inn* and a hotel with an unspecified name at High Harrogate; and *The Crown*, *White Hart*, *Crescent* and *The Swan* in Low Harrogate. The accommodation they provided was augmented by a host of lodging houses. A 'Tourist's Companion' published in this year gave details of attractions that might be visited from Harrogate in a day, including Fountains Abbey, Studley Park, Hackfall, Brimham Crags, Newby Hall, Harewood House, Bolton Abbey and, of course, historic Knaresborough.

In the twilight period of Harrogate as a spa in the classical Regency sense, Henry Curling wrote of a time when some of the hotels were 'fully-blown posting houses' with accommodation for thirty carriages and stabling for a hundred horses. At these posting houses, coaches were not only serviced and teams exchanged but fresh carriage and postillions could be hired. 'Along the turnpike roads which bisected the noble greensward of the Stray, the grinding, rolling team of coach and horses would move, all groaning wood, creaking leather, jingling brass, steaming horses and impatient passengers, accompanied no doubt by a crowd of urchins taking good care to keep out of reach of the coachman's whip and the turning wheels of the great vehicle.' Curling thought the arrival of one of the Harrogate stages, such as the splendidly named *Rocket*, *Dart*, *True Briton*, *Tally-ho* or *Teazle*, must have been 'a sight to quicken the pulse of the most seasoned spa visitor'. He was to recall the 'days of romance and nights of revelry and excitement at the major hotels'. They were often referred to by nickname: *The Dragon* was 'The House of Commons' and *The Granby* had become 'The House of Lords'. The *Queen's*

54 The first Corporation drivers outside the stables in Market Square, 1882.

Head was referred to as 'Manchester Warehouse' and *The Crown*'s curious nickname was 'The Hospital'. The implication was that the *Granby* was for the posh or, as Curling observed, 'the most staid and straight-laced and the invalided portions of the aristocracy'. More sporting types converged on *The Dragon*: 'There the sporting gentry of the day, the great turf men', mixed with a sprinkling of the aristocracy and the old country families, 'together with parties from the north: Highland lairds and rollicking blades from the Emerald Isle'. These met annually and kept up a continued revel during the season. *The Crown*, as its nickname suggested, was where the sick tended to stay, being handy for the wells of Low Harrogate. The *Queen's Head*, 'a long, irregular built Scotch-looking mansion', standing almost opposite *The Granby*, earned its name because it was mostly tenanted 'by the trading portion of the company'—the Manchester textile men and well-to-do

pinmakers from Birmingham, 'the wealthy cutler from Sheffield, the iron-founder from Black Barnsley, the clothier from Leeds and the moneyed man from Glasgow, Dundee and Paisley', who would feel uneasy in the company of the old-rich patronising the major hotels.

Curling also described 'a devoted son of the clergy, one of the finest preachers of the day', who sermonised in the morning on the enormity of gaming then clambered into his curricle and drove to *The Dragon*, there to 'pass the entire remainder of the sabbath behind the closed blinds of the card-room, absorbed body and soul in whist, or setting the fee-simple of his living upon a turn of the dice-box'. A rich Indian nabob had 'successively lost three fortunes at Harrogate, Cheltenham and Buxton'. An unidentified lady who died at the card-table 'would at times have her lap filled with banknotes, which she had no leisure to count. This lady was wont to play frequently

VICTORIA
Public Baths,
HARROGATE,

The Property of the Harrogate Corporation.

ERECTED AT A COST OF £30,000.

These Magnificent Baths are supplied with water from upwards of

THIRTY MILD AND STRONG

SULPHUR SPRINGS

First Class Hot Sulphur Baths 2s. each, or twelve for 20s.
Second Class   do   1s. 6d. „   „   15s.
Vapour, Needle, Shower, Ascending and Descending Douche Baths, &c.

Open from 7 a.m. to 8 p.m., Week-days; 8 a.m to 1 p.m. on Sundays,
By Order,
W. HENRY WYLES, Town Clerk.

ROYAL PUMP ROOM AND MINERAL SPRINGS,
HARROGATE;

THE principal Wells and Springs of Harrogate, the valuable medical qualities of which are well-known, are the property of the Harrogate Corporation, by whom they are strictly conserved, and under whose regulations they are supplied to the public—

At the Pump Room, Low Harrogate.
   „   **Tewit Well, High Harrogate.**
   „   **Magnesia Well, Bogs Field.**
   „   **John's Well, High Harrogate.**

Handbooks may be obtained, written by eminent local medical gentlemen, giving the analyses and medical properties of the various springs.

55 An advertisement for the Victoria Public Baths, from *Thorpe's Illustrated Guide to Harrogate*, 1886.

for a cool hundred a game and at the same time bet with those near her table.'

A change of emphasis occurred when John Williams, arriving in Harrogate in the 1830s, bought a plot behind the Promenade Room and constructed the Victoria Baths. Its arrival set the scene for the future development of Harrogate. Curling observed that a new race sprang up: 'Mirth and jollity seemed banished … The card-room was deserted, the billiard-rooms were empty; and although there seemed a decent sprinkling of guests at the hotels, compared with the choice and master spirits of former times, the assemblage was a quaker's meeting …' The number of annual visitors to Harrogate rose from 1,556 in 1781 to 2,486 by 1795. The figure doubled again to 5,858 in 1810, when the local population was about 1,500. Low Harrogate became respectable, especially after 1805 when Lord Byron stayed at *The Crown*, and in 1808, when the Old Sulphur Well was covered by an elegant pillared structure, along the lines of a Roman temple. It was deduced that Tuscan columns would not violate the award enclosing The Stray, which had specified that no new walls should be added. A single acre of the Bog's Field (now the Valley Gardens) was found to have 36 mineral springs, each distinctive, thus ensuring the continuing prosperity of the area.

Chapter Five

Victorian Grandeur

Modern Harrogate is largely a Victorian creation. The town had a rapid increase in population from the beginning of the 19th century. In 1801, the townships of Bilton with Harrogate and Pannal, which took in Beckwith with Rossett, were home to 1,984 people. Thirty years later, this figure had risen to 4,073, with an appreciable number of young male workers having jobs connected with farming. Visitors were impressed by the many stylish buildings and by the spaciousness of the urban layout. In the 1820s, those frequenting The Stray saw grazing animals, notably cows, and had to be careful where they were placing their feet. In 1822, a sulphur spring was located where the Thackwray family grazed a horse and was commercially exploited. A pump house was constructed in the Chinese style and the area laid out as a garden. Naturally, there was a small charge for admission.

The Harrogate Act of 1841 and the appointment of 21 Commissioners charged with the 'improvement' of High and Low Harrogate ensured that development would be both rapid and orderly. To qualify as a Commissioner, a man had to be a rent-payer of £35 or a property owner of £20 a year. The seven men who were obliged to retire each April were replaced by others elected by a paper-vote. The Improvement Commissioners worked well; they certainly ensured that from 1841 until 1884, when Harrogate became a borough council, there was little or no unseemly development.

In stark contrast to the Georgian village noted for its mineral wells, by 1841, when the first Commissioners were elected, Sydney Smith could peevishly observe, after brief acquaintance with Harrogate, that the inn-keepers charge 'London prices' and were, in effect, 'lords of the place'; while the Old Sulphur Well had as its attendants 'ragged women who exist on charity'. He categorised the visitors as either snobbish 'ha-ha-ing' aristocrats or upstart north-country manufacturers. The flower-beds and neat gardens were attractive. The 'lords of Harrogate' could be discriminating about whom they admitted to their hotels. Edmund Bogg quoted in his book *From Eden Vale to the Plains of York*:

> Through Knaresborough I pass'd, from that field of renown
> And arriv'd safe at Harrowgate—drove to the Crown;
> I inquir'd for two rooms—heard them quickly declare
> The house was so full, they'd not one room to spare;
> Then I drove to the Crescent and then the White Hart;
> But they each, my dear fellow, performed the same part.
> The reason did, afterwards, plainly appear:
> 'Twas because I'd no servant attending me there.

The visitor was eventually accommodated in a boarding house.

Harrogate's main streets resounded to the passage of stage-coaches, which drew up outside one of the town's four coaching inns amid a flurry of activity as travellers disembarked and teams of horses were replaced. A coach service connected Harrogate with Newcastle, York, Leeds and Selby. At the last-named place, a traveller might transfer to one of the daily steam packets sailing to Hull. A journey that began in Harrogate might end, with little inconvenience apart from the stresses of travel itself, with a crossing of the North Sea to the Low Countries. The *True Blue* coach operated between Knaresborough and Selby until 1835. The service was replaced by a coach to Micklefield, where those bound for Hull continued their journey to Selby by train. The *Harrogate Advertiser* of September 1838 has details of 18 daily departures by stage-coach. A through service to Newcastle and Manchester was available. Anyone who was bound for Leeds paid 4s. for an inside seat and 2s. or 2s. 6d. to travel outside on the 16-mile journey. The outsiders stoically endured three hours' exposure

to whatever the weather threw at them. Horse-drawn vehicles of all kinds, ranging from trades-men's outfits to the smart stage-coaches, were such a feature of Harrogate that, by 1822, two local firms specialised in coach-building.

Road improvements in the 1820s and 1830s included an easier route over Blubber-houses Moor to Skipton, the avoidance of a steep ascent of Brimham Moor on the way to Pateley Bridge in Nidderdale, and an easing of gradients on the road from Harrogate to mid-

Wharfedale. Carriages drawn by sleek horses took visitors from the better hotels to local beauty spots. The aforementioned Granville, in the first volume of *The Spas of England* (1841), noted that before the end of July 'carts and gigs empty their gatherings daily. Coroneted chariots, britzsckas and post-chaises ply about in abundance after that, bringing their more noble cargoes of aristocratic visitors.' Already the whistle of the steam locomotive was being heard in the land, though, and before

56   The old Harrogate railway station.

57 Harrogate Railway Station.

58 A diesel passenger train crossing the viaduct over the Nidd at Knaresborough.

59   Harrogate New Baths.

long some horse-drawn coaches that called at Harrogate connected with the Leeds-Selby railway. As an example of the high mobility now available, in 1842 a daily coach from Harrogate took travellers via Knaresborough and Boroughbridge to the railway station at Thirsk. The coach left Harrogate at 9.15 a.m. so as to connect with the 12.33 train to Darlington and Newcastle. The coach then met the south-bound train at 4.30 and the round trip ended in Harrogate at 7.00 p.m.

It was during the 60 glorious years of Victoria's reign, which began in 1837, that Harrogate eclipsed Knaresborough and, indeed, many of the other spas in the land. Harrogate's successful exploitation of its mineral wells was to the detriment of communities where similar features existed. For example, at Starbeck, the in-between community, sulphur and chalybeate springs had been patronised in the 17th and 18th centuries, but by the dawn of the 19th they were being ignored. Michael Calvert, a Knaresborough druggist, asserted that their neglect had been caused by rival interests and in particular by a Dr. Murray. At a public meeting held in Knaresborough in March 1822, a committee was appointed to raise subscriptions so that Starbeck Old Spa might be restored, which it was, now re-named Knaresborough Spa as it was on land that formed part of that town. Starbeck opened public baths in 1828, raising the cost by issuing shares. The income was to cover running expenses so there would be no dividend for the investors.

Extended a few years later, the enterprise was renowned for its facilities, comprising four warm baths, two shower baths and a cold plunge. Improvements continued to be made and in the early 1840s additional supplies of sulphur water became available.

Harrogate's importance as a spa, however, was undiminished. The Old Sulphur Well had been provided with a handsome cupola, and a Promenade Room, 75 ft. long and 30 ft. wide, was available from 1805 to shelter and entertain those imbibing the waters when the weather was poor. The Room also provided a venue for meetings and concerts. Two new springs, one a chalybeate and the other of saline iron, were found in Low Harrogate. A small pump room was constructed over the second spring, which became known as the Cheltenham Saline after a Dr. Adam Hunter, who described the two springs in 1819, erroneously compared the water with that in the West Country spa town. The success of the Victoria Baths, which gave the owner a good financial return and were popular with visitors, prompted the Thackwray family, of

The Crown, who also had a 'pleasure ground', to devote part of the land to the construction of competing baths. With architecture of the Greek-revival style, these were opened in 1834 and became known as the Montpellier or Crown Baths. They were also successful. Bathing took place in luxurious surroundings and under medical supervision.

Each of the major hotels of Harrogate developed a distinctive style and all contributed to the Season. In June 1811, reported the *York Herald*, 'this celebrated watering place is assuming its wonted gaiety. Every day brings considerable additions to the number of fashionables; and it is expected that in a short time, the inns and lodging houses will be crowded with the first families of the United Kingdom.' The newspaper instanced *The Granby* and its 'sumptuous entertainment ... in honour of the Prince Regent's special gala'. Dancing began at 10 o'clock, 'and about two, the company (amongst whom beauty, elegance and fashion conspicuously shone) partook of an elegant repast.' The party ended about 4 a.m.

60   An engraving of Victoria Baths, 1872.

61 Victoria Baths which now, significantly altered, are Council offices.

During the 1820s and 1830s, the Duchy of Lancaster developed its Harrogate estates, providing high quality housing in a neat and attractive scheme. The Duchy also allocated land for a church, which was built in Low Harrogate, freeing churchgoers from the necessity of travelling to Pannal, in which parish this part of Harrogate was situated. Joseph Thackwray and his family took a keen interest in the church that was built on the Esplanade, near the junction with Cold Bath Road. At High Harrogate, which was originally in the parish of Knaresborough, Duchy co-operation enabled the construction of Christ Church, which in 1831 replaced the Chapel of St John, a small building in a state of disrepair. The church arose on a triangular island of The Stray. A memorial tablet affixed on the north side of the extended Christ Church commemorates W.P. Frith, who became widely known as a painter of large and busy scenes such as 'Derby Day' and 'Ramsgate Sands'. The Friths were a notable churchgoing family, who presided over *The Dragon*. One of the vicars, P.F.D. de

Labbiliere, was to become Bishop Suffragan of Knaresborough and Dean of Westminster.

In 1826, Lord Harewood provided land in Cornwall Road (then known as Bogs Lane) for the Bath Hospital, a charitable organisation catering for the poor who lived over three miles away. Among the original donations was fifty guineas from King George IV. The hospital succeeded a charitable fund for poor patients that was sustained by contributions from hotels and lodging houses. Initially, the Bath Hospital had 25 patients, a number that rose to 45 by 1838. The hospital was not open during the main season, for the trust did not wish to antagonise the benefactors who had business interests in visitors. At that time of year, all the sulphur water flowing from the springs of Bogs Field was made available to the gentry and other notable visitors, who in any case could not be brought into sight, much less contact, with the poor. Pickersgill Pallister, the honorary secretary of the hospital, stimulated the townsfolk's interest in their paying guests when he began to publish a list of visitors to

62 Christ Church, Park Parade, from an engraving of 1853. The church was built in 1829 and the transepts and chancel were added in 1861.

63 The Royal Bath Hospital from Valley Gardens. The hospital was opened in 1889 by Prince Albert, Duke of Clarence.

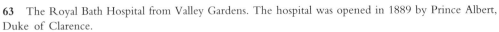

64   Lithograph of the Cheltenham Pump Room, Harrogate Wells.

Harrogate. To these, in due course, were added details of entertainment and a few advertisements, including one for bottled Harrogate water. The idea had, by 1836, burgeoned into the *Harrogate Advertiser*, the town's first newspaper. This was a boom year for Harrogate, but the buoyant economic conditions did not last and in the following year a trade depression caused the number of visitors to fall. By 1843, when Harrogate might be visited in a day by train or coach from as far away as London and Tyneside, a slow recovery of numbers was being experienced, the first of a series of Annual Flower Shows was held in the grounds of the Cheltenham Spa and the local boom continued, the Band playing 'every evening in the season' on the Green at High Harrogate in 1845. Another trade dip occurred in 1848 and the businessmen of Harrogate again tightened their belts.

John Williams, keen to augment the income from his Victoria Baths, acquired the site of newly-discovered springs, including that named after Cheltenham, and requested his architect, Mr. Clarke, to design a large building that would incorporate pump and drinking facilities and also a vast assembly room. In August 1835, the Royal Promenade and Cheltenham Pump Room (later known as The Spa Rooms) were brought into use with a public ball. Those attending found the area brilliantly illuminated and passed through a Doric-style portico to enter a building constructed in the shape of a Greek temple. The Band of the Scots Greys performed. Next evening, fireworks blazed in the night sky. A weekly subscription in 1838-9 cost 3s. 6d. per person, with a special rate of 10s. for a family. The charges had been raised a shilling by 1842, the new price including admission to concerts that were held nightly. Williams also acquired six acres of land behind the building and they became pleasure grounds, with walks on two levels. He had the beck dammed, creating what Dr. Granville described as 'the prettiest spot in Harrogate'. Boating took place on a lake that was somewhat narrow for its length and was also grossly polluted, the beck having acted as a sewer for Low Harrogate and dealing with waste water from the sulphur baths. All this happened at a time when a serious decline in the Knaresborough linen industry had led to the closing-down of Harrogate's many bleach-yards.

Joseph Holdsworth, a Leeds man who, in 1837, bought some neglected buildings at the Harrogate Cold Bath, arranged for the construction of a big lodging house 'with suitable bathing rooms'. The enterprise was named St Magnus and Holdsworth charged one shilling for the use of 'plunging, shower and spouting baths'. By 1839, Harrogate had over 150 hotels and lodging houses. The average of the weekly lists published in the *Harrogate Advertiser* for the period June-October was 20,586, which was thought to be exceeded by no German spa except possibly Carlsbad. The

figure for Harrogate did not take into account early and late visitors, such as the titled and/or wealthy folk and their servants.

Six years before the Improvement Act was introduced, the hotelier Joseph Thackwray, while looking for additional supplies of sulphur water for his new baths, sank a well under a shop he owned. It was only 50 feet from the Old Sulphur Well. His action violated the Forest of Knaresborough Enclosure Act of 1770, which forbade the sinking of any pit 'whereby the said medicinal springs ... may be damaged, polluted or affected'. Thackwray refused to abandon his digging. Rival hoteliers were among those who met in the Promenade Room and decided to prosecute him. A long case reached its climax at York Assizes in March 1837, when there was a compromise settlement, Thackwray agreeing to allow the public free access to the water. A small steam engine was installed to pump water from several springs. Montpellier, the grand-sounding name of a celebrated French spa, was selected by Thackwray to distinguish his new baths. A keen competitor to the nearby Cheltenham establishment of John Williams, he supplied an annual six thousand spa treatments to his rival's four thousand.

65 An engraving of Montpellier Springs and Baths, 1857. The Baths were built by Joseph Thackwray in 1835 but were replaced by the Royal Baths and Winter Gardens in 1897.

66 Montpellier Baths, *c.*1860.

67 Montpellier Gardens in the late 19th century.

68   Valley Gardens in 1926.

Joseph Thackwray died in April 1837. His well was neglected, and it was discovered that his widow was tapping it with a pipe, which she was ordered to disconnect. Within a short time of Thackwray's passing, his great rival, Williams, had also died. In 1839, those who had set up the Victoria Company bought the old Promenade Rooms and Williams's Baths, which became the Victoria Baths. Thomas Gordon leased the Cheltenham Pump Room and Gardens from the executors of John Williams. (Montpellier Baths and estate were purchased by Harrogate Council in 1888 for

£29,000 and in 1897 the Royal Baths were opened on the site.)

The toll income for the turnpike road between Harrogate and Leeds around 1840 was over £450 a mile, which implies it was one of the busiest in Yorkshire. The Improvement Commissioners met for the first time in July 1841 and applied themselves to the work of improvement, despite their limited powers. They had what became known as the Royal Pump House constructed, to a design by Isaac Shutt. There was a whiff of scandal, for Shutt had family connections with the owners of *The*

Swan and, after he had been given the work four Commissioners, suspecting favouritism, promptly resigned. Two of them, having made a strong representation, accepted re-election. One was Nicholas Carter, who was making a name for himself in the building industry, and was destined to become the first mayor. Incidentally, the Commissioners arranged for public access to the sulphur waters to be by purchase or subscription; a free supply was (and still is) available outside the building.

When the Pump Room was opened, the women who had attended the wells for over a century found themselves out of work. They had been described by Thomas Baskerville: 'Their faces did shine like bacon rind. And for beauty may vie with an old Bath guide's ass, the sulphur waters had so fouled their pristine complexions.' The legendary Elizabeth Lupton, much better known as Betty Lupton, Queen of Harrogate, attended the springs for 56 years. An old account of her states she was 'a privileged person' who 'dispenses the waters and quodlibets with equal liberality'. Betty dipped into the spring with a long-handled horn spoon and distributed the sulphurous drink to those who rose from their beds early, quaffed dutifully and then walked off the effects of this

69 The Royal Pump Room, Old Sulphur Well, was erected in 1842 from a design by Isaac Shutt and cost £3,000 to build. It has been a museum since 1953.

70 & 71 Views of the Royal Pump Room, Old Sulphur Well, proliferated. Engravings were succeeded by picture postcards.

72 Attending to the roof of the Pump Room. On the left is the entrance to the Valley Gardens.

73 The interior of the Pump Room.

74 Betty Lupton, an attendent at the Old Sulphur Well, who was pronounced the 'Queen of Harrogate'.

75 Sarah Gamp, expressing distaste at the sulphur water.

natural medicine by promenading the Bogs Field. In August 1843, when she was old and frail and employed by the Harrogate Improvement Commissioners, Betty was granted an allowance of a shilling a day. She did not draw this pension for long and died in 1845.

Gas lighting came to Harrogate in 1847 but, as usual, there was much wrangling and argument. The candlemakers were quick to point out their loss of trade. The Commissioners were unhappy about the price the gas company charged, which led to the supply being cut off for an appreciable period. Dr. Kennion, in a letter published in the *Harrogate Advertiser* of 16 May 1849, pleaded for unity and a desire to work together to further the real interests of

the town. He added, 'The people are all too busy quarrelling among themselves to have any time or attention to throw away upon visitors.' Despite squabbling, however, the spa town was prospering and private enterprises ensured for visitors a good selection of hotels and boarding houses, plus up-to-date medical attention and various diversions.

There were, by now, two weekly newspapers, the *Harrogate Advertiser* and *Harrogate Herald*, the first reflecting Conservative and the second more radical points of view. From the year 1847, when journalists from each newspaper were reporting on meetings of the Commissioners, we have a full and accurate account of their activities.

The disposal of sewage and provision of additional supplies of fresh water were other matters in hand. A police force was required to replace the Constable, a grocer who did the work part-time and could not cope with the problems that arose during a crowded Season. Police were much in evidence during the 14 years from 1848, when the railways were being built by navvies who tended to go wild with strong drink in their leisure time. The railways, though, were a godsend to Harrogate, which had suffered in the early 1840s from a wider trade recession and was also recording a quite steep decline in the stage-coach services. The arrival of the first railway in 1848 did not appeal to everyone. Farm folk considered that steam engines, breathing smoke and sparks, would frighten their stock. Others were conscious that trains would also bring to town masses of working-class folk from the West Riding industrial towns—folk who would bring their own food, consume it out-of-doors and generally lower the tone of the place. The offer of the Leeds and Thirsk Railway Company to run their main line through Harrogate was narrowly turned down at a town's meeting, which decided it should approach no nearer than Starbeck. Even before the Starbeck line was built, a proposal of the York and North Midland Railway Company to end its branch line from Church Fenton, via Wetherby, near the Spa was approved, and a wooden station appeared on a site near the *Brunswick*, which became the *Prince of Wales*.

An enterprise of the celebrated George Hudson, the York and North Midland Railway involved the construction of a huge viaduct across the Crimple valley. At Harrogate, the Brunswick station was opened for traffic on 20 July 1848. Happily for the company, the Tewit Well was unaffected by the excavations, for the Commissioners insisted that, if the celebrated well had been harmed, another well should be found and equipped. The East and West Yorkshire Junction Railway from York was extended to the east side of Knaresborough.

76 Dickinson's the greengrocers.

The railway brought day-trippers by the thousand. On 3 July 1850, a train of 54 carriages, containing over 2,000 people from the Sheffield area, drew into Brunswick station. The *Harrogate Advertiser* noted that 'the road down West Park and Parliament Street presented one dense moving mass of human beings, wending their way towards the Cheltenham Spa Rooms, where a great number partook of tea in the afternoon.' So novel was the arrival by rail of this crowd of strangers that many Harrogate people converged on Brunswick station at 6.30 p.m. to watch the train depart.

In 1862, the Brunswick terminus in High Harrogate was dismantled (its site is now marked by a stone on The Stray near Trinity Methodist Church). The Central Station had come into operation under the auspices of the North Eastern Company, which had absorbed the two earlier companies and constructed a loop line connecting with the main line, north and south, at Bilton and the Crimple Viaduct, and joining up with the York line at Starbeck. This gave Harrogate a new centre of gravity and led to a rapid growth of property and population in Low Harrogate, new houses being sited on the north side of the valley, where they were handy both for the spa and the railway station. With speedy rail links with Bradford or Leeds, commuting was possible for the businessman. After a day in office or factory, what better than to embark on a train that would take him to wife and children, comfortably housed in a villa situated in a leafy road at Harrogate? The closing of Brunswick station led to open ground lying south-west of The Stray being developed with numerous small mansions. At the same time, two small parks (the ovals) were created by the West End Park Company. The Duchy of Lancaster had land in plenty and developed the Dragon and Lancaster Park estates. The building boom that brought into being Terraces, Places and Courts galore was sustained by numerous handy quarries, which reduced transport costs for stone, and by the brick-

77 From a recent issue of the *Harrogate Advertiser*.

works established to the south and east of the expanding town. These self-same quarries were exceedingly busy when a building boom gave rise to properties grouped in Avenues, Groves and Crescents.

By developing as a tourist town, Harrogate became a paradise for hypochondriacs. A visitors' handbook of 1858 included advertisements for W. Hardy, Professor of Medico-Electricity, who subjected a patient, strapped to a chair or sitting in a bath, to a mild electric shock. Mr. Mosely was a surgeon–dentist who had invented 'terreous artificial teeth, without springs, wires or fastenings'. The 'wind pills' of Page Woodcock would cure almost anything you cared to think of, from wind in stomach and bowels to skin eruptions. The bracing air and a modicum of exercise were probably just as helpful! If fresh air alone was required, a bath-chair might be hired at 1s. 3d. an hour or a cab used, the type drawn by a single horse costing a shilling a mile and by two horses at five shillings for a whole hour. *Thorpe's Illustrated Guide to Harrogate* (1886) carried an advertisement for The Imperial Sanatorium and Winter Residence for invalids and visitors, which now, under new management, had been much altered and improved, offering medical electricity: 'In addition to the usual treatment of diseases, invalids suffering from chronic complaints can be treated here by the scientific application of electricity.' Also available was a variety of baths—Turkish, Spray, Douche and Hydropathic.

When, in 1855, news was received that Sebastopol in the Crimea had fallen and a messy war appeared to be over, Harrogate celebrated by firing a royal salute of 21 guns. Local people processed through the town. *The Crown* laid out tables and filled them with food for which no charge was made. The 'labouring classes' were informed that knives, forks and plates would be provided. Anyone who attended need bring only an appetite. After the feasting came sports, with wheelbarrow races taking place down Cold Bath Lane. The highlight of the

78 Announcement of 1886.

celebrations came with the storming of a 'Russian tower' that had been packed with combustibles. An estimated 8,000 people watched its incineration. There were cheers for Queen Victoria and also for the Emperor of France, whose country had been allied with Britain in the Crimea.

Richard Ellis, a self-made man who was elected as an Improvement Commissioner in 1855, was a dominant figure in Victorian Harrogate. He laboured hard and long for the benefit of the town, striving for the adoption of the Local Government Act, 1858. He founded Ashville School, supported the

79   Richard Ellis, Mayor of Harrogate, 1884-7.

80   Alderman Charles Fortune, Mayor of Harrogate, 1893-5 (see Chapter Seven).

establishment of a cottage hospital and, just as significant for good health, an effective sewage system. It was he who proposed, when a new central railway station was required to join up the lines from Leeds and Knaresborough, that the line should be put in a cutting out of sight, and the loss of land to The Stray be compensated by adding the site of the old Brunswick station. There were mutterings by the public who found they could reach the station only from the west. In due course (this might have been the motto of Harrogate at the time) Richard Ellis built a road, East Parade, in 1875, and thus solved the problem of access to the station. The road was his gift

to the town but, not missing a commercial opportunity, he built some stone houses on the west side.

Celebrities were happy to be noticed at Harrogate. William Wordsworth and Robert Southey brought a breath of Lake District air to the town. Charles Dickens was here in September 1858, and gave public readings in the Spa Rooms, expressing himself happy with the financial return and commenting that Harrogate was 'the queerest place, with the strangest people in it'. They were leading 'the oddest lives of dancing, newspaper reading, and tables d'hôte'. At his reading of *Little Dorritt*, one gentleman was reduced to tears, presumably because he had lost a child.

Chapter Six

Victorian Borough

Harrogate came of age in a flurry of building work, much of which was stimulated by the construction of the central railway station. The infilling of Central Harrogate began. The commercial importance of High Harrogate waned on account of the long delay in providing a road that was handy for the new station. Five of the first seven mayors of the town were concerned with building. Not all of those who set out to make a fortune from stone and mortar were successful. Joshua Bower, who in 1855 bought the *Dragon Hotel* and 53 acres of land for £11,500, reckoned that a proposal to build a station near the hotel on a line that was planned from Starbeck to High Harrogate, and a new road to link it with Low Harrogate, would enhance the value of his property. The station was constructed elsewhere and the road did not take shape until after Bower's death. His Dragon estate suffered from the presence of a railway on an embankment which rendered it unsuitable for the best type of development. (Not until 1892 would the estate be fully developed.) When, in 1860, Richard Ellis and the Carter brothers formed the Victoria Park Company, with a capital of £28,000, enough to buy a large tract of land close to the station site, a splendid thorough-fare called Victoria Avenue was constructed to link High Harrogate at Queen Parade with Low Harrogate at West Park. The properties were soundly constructed of local stone and the various designs for dwellings were harmonious. George Dawson, another local builder,

set his men to work on what would become Montpellier Parade. Men like Ellis and Dawson impressed the townsfolk with quality work and made themselves rich in the process.

Harrogate's central station was open for use in August 1862. The main shopping centre was now to be found in close proximity to the station: in Chapel Street, which was later to be called Oxford Street, and in Parliament Street and James Street. In 1865, the last-named thoroughfare became the venue for the main post office, which had previously stood in High Harrogate. The railway offered an excellent service, the fastest trains connecting the town with Leeds in 45 minutes and with London in six-and-a-half hours. Such a service persuaded people to visit the town and tempted middle-class folk living in the sooted suburbs of West Riding industrial towns such as Bradford and Leeds to move their families to leafy Harrogate. George Rogers, for example, was a Bradford millowner with poor health, who moved to Harrogate and in 1868 used some of his considerable fortune to build almshouses for needy but respectable women, some from Bradford and others from Harrogate. The last link in the railway system came with the opening of the Harrogate-Pateley Bridge branch. At Pateley, in the upper valley of the Nidd, the terminus was a single platform. George Dawson, a forthright man who had earlier played in the modest role of a cooper, took out a mortgage on Ashfield House, where the Thackwray family had lived, and proceeded

81 Oxford Street, *c.*1900. The thoroughfare was originally called Chapel Street.

82 James Street from Station Square, with a view of Standings Grocery and Café, which was a familiar local feature for many years.

83   The elegant buildings in James Street.

84   James Street, a Victorian engraving by E.G. Fenton.

85 Prospect Place and the *Prospect Hotel*. The hotel was built in 1859.

to develop the rest of the estate, employing J.H. Hirst as his architect. It was a splendid collaboration that brought into being some of the town's finest buildings: part of Parliament Street, Cambridge and Prospect Crescents and some stylish villas at West End Park. Sparks flew when Dawson and the Improvement Commissioners disagreed about some of his plans, and continued to fly when, in 1870, Dawson became one of that influential group.

The Commissioners adopted the Local Government Act of 1858 four years after it had passed through Parliament and became the Board of Health at a time when untreated sewage was being discharged into the becks, with nauseous consequences in the heat of summer. The Act permitted the Commissioners to borrow up to £30,000 but they worked frugally, in the manner of good Yorkshiremen. When the rate was set at sixpence in the pound,

86 *Prospect Hotel* and the Stray.

87 View from West Park.

some of their ratepayers accused them of extravagance. In 1862, the Commissioners drove a road from the Royal Pump Room to the springs of Bogs Field and in the following year they arranged for flagstones to be laid on what were at that time referred to as sidewalks. From 1862, their every achievement was being chronicled in the local press, which became a continuous rather than just a seasonal occurrence. Regular publication came at a formative time for Harrogate. During the thirty years from the 1860s to the 1890s, the town experienced a trebling of both the population and the number of houses.

Richard Ellis was scarcely ever out of the news, losing his seat on the local authority in 1871, but regaining it in the following year. The cause of disquiet had been the construction of yet another suite of baths, for which, as a prominent local citizen, Ellis laid the foundation stone. Too much public 'brass' was being thrown about. Standing beside the Old Victoria Baths, the project became the New Victoria Baths, and featured a spacious entrance hall, smaller treatment rooms and bathing pools, one for men and the other for women. Despite their complexity, the New Victoria Baths were constructed and brought into use in a single year, 1871, taking sulphur water from springs on the site and from the majority of the springs in Bogs Field then storing it in reservoirs beneath the building.

The most direct route between High Harrogate and Low Harrogate remained a field path on which, at busy times, people queued at stiles. Wheeled traffic had to follow one of two roundabout routes that had scarcely outgrown their ancient status of country lanes. At long last, in 1871, the Commissioners were legally able to borrow enough money to finance a new road between the two parts of the town, the scheme having been a topic of lively, often acrimonious, debate for almost a quarter of a century. In 1875, traffic began to use an upgraded Bower Road. A branch road led to the rear of the railway station. Acrimony also

attended discussion of a market, the absence of which was noticeable in a town of Harrogate's size. After much procrastination, which delighted the hawkers, a market was provided in 1874 at a cost of £3,600 (exclusive of land). Arthur Hiscoe, a local architect, designed the scheme and on the opening day, 30 August, the band of the Harrogate Rifle Volunteers provided joyous strains. Henry Greensmith and George Dawson, who were respectively chairmen of the Commissioners and of the Market Committee, gave the obligatory speeches. The available market stalls were taken up within a week and soon more stalls were required.

The cost of the timepiece in the clock tower—a timepiece made by Potts of Leeds—was defrayed by the Baroness Burdett-Coutts, who was not only a regular visitor to Harrogate but reputedly second only to the Queen in the list of the country's richest women. Her wealth was derived from her father, one of the wealthy Coutts family, and from the second marriage of her mother, who had become the Duchess of St Albans. One of the speakers at a celebratory dinner remarked, 'Harrogate has made its way in spite of its inhabitants'.

At about this time, some of the Commissioners appear to have been directors of private utilities, such as gas and water, hence their reluctance to take these over. In 1872, the gas company was charging a swingeing £664 for the gas used for street lighting. Coal brought to Starbeck station was transported to the gasworks in wagons drawn by steam traction engines which breathed clouds of acrid smoke into what was being advertised as fresh air. The worst sufferers were those in the posh hotels and houses of High Harrogate. Another charge levied against the traction engines was that they scared 'nervous individuals and high-spirited horses'. In fairness to the gas company, there had been a steep rise in the cost of coal and economies of a sort had been made. Poorer quality coal saved money but increased the pollution. Another cost-saving and highly-imaginative scheme was not to bring the street lights into use on moonlit nights. Indoor gas lighting was generally poor, one shopkeeper lamenting that at times he had difficulty in distinguishing a sixpence from a half sovereign. When, in 1880, a takeover seemed likely, the gas company found fresh capital and built rail sidings at Bilton Junction, re-routing the offensive traction engines away from the area of the Spa.

Rail travellers at Harrogate had a favoured time. For only £15 a year, a commuter to Leeds might acquire a first-class season ticket and have the choice of a dozen trains daily each way, a number that increased to 16, then to 18 as the Victorian period evolved. The trains used by businessmen covered the distance to Leeds in no more than 40 minutes. The rail service to Bradford, via Otley and Shipley, had risen to eight trains a day by the 1890s, the journey time being about 50 minutes. By the start of the 20th century, a businessman commuting from Harrogate to Bradford who was prepared to pay rather more than the standard rate was able to travel in a special 'club saloon'.

Harrogate had become a conspicuously religious place. It was fashionable to go to church. For Anglicans, largely comprising the middle class, St John's was built at Bilton in 1857, followed by the construction of St Peter's near the new centre of the town. The work began in 1871 and was completed five years later (a tower appearing, almost as an

88 & 89 St Peter's Church and a detail from the stained glass window commemorating the dead of the First World War. It features a cartoon of the Unknown Soldier from the magazine *Punch*.

afterthought, in the 1920s). At Christ Church, in 1875, Dr. E.H. Bickersteth, Bishop of Exeter, having heard Canon Gibbon preach on a text from Isaiah, went outdoors, scanned the broad acres of The Stray and composed the hymn 'Peace, perfect Peace'. The Roman Catholics had built St Robert's Church in 1873. John Wesley rode into the area in 1788, as can be seen from a plaque at the chapel in Hillfoot Lane, near Pannal. Methodism was soon established and expanded rapidly. Wesley Chapel, which had a central situation, was completed in 1862 at a cost of £4,000. Trinity Methodist Church, one of the outstanding Victorian Gothic structures, was opened on The Stray in 1878, having cost £11,000. The spire of this building seems to extend half-way to heaven. The Congregationalists built an impressive church in 1862 and the Baptists had a worthy focal point in the place of worship that was completed in 1883. The Church was also a pioneer in educational development. Of the many schools founded in the wave of Victorian piety and desire for self-improvement, a few

remain, among them Ashville College, a residential school for boys, founded by Wesleyans who had bought the high ground at Pannal Ash in 1877. Ashville attained the status of a public school, having absorbed New College, on Leadhall Lane (and is now, like many another, co-ed). Oatlands, a preparatory school established at the edge of The Stray in 1881, moved to Goldsborough Hall.

Harrogate was incorporated as a borough in 1884. Those who objected to the proposals were thinking mainly of the likelihood of an increase in rates. Yet, when the Charter of Incorporation reached the town by train it was warmly welcomed. The crack of fog detonators placed on the track was heard above the massed cheers. A procession of carriages bore the Charter and notable citizens to the New Victoria Baths, where a dais had been erected and congratulatory speeches were made. The town adopted as its motto *Arx Celebris Fontibus* ('The centre [or citadel] famous for its springs'). The Borough occupied the province that had been governed by the Commissioners and was

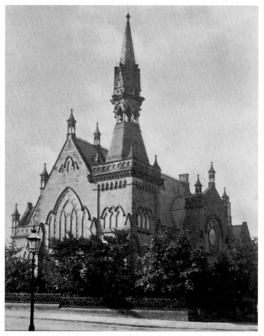

90 Victoria Park United Methodist Free Church, built in 1865 but now demolished.

91 Victorian Avenue Congregational Church, West Park Stray in *c*.1890.

92 Christ Church, which stands on a triangular island of the Stray, having replaced the Chapel of St John.

93 Ashville College, of Methodist origin, is situated at almost the highest point in Harrogate. The main buildings are viewed from land that subsequently became a cricket pitch.

now divided into three wards—East, West and Central—each ward having six councillors. Six aldermen were appointed and the offices of the new body were in the Victoria Baths building, which had been built by the Commissioners.

The town's reputation as a spa depended on its ability to keep up-to-date with facilities and treatment. In Austria, the cult of hydropathy, developed in the 1820s, was based on cold water, no less, without any mineral content, and associated with mountainside activity. When the new cult was brought to England, it was Malvern, not Harrogate, that adopted it. Then, in 1846, a hydropathic hotel with a range of baths and facilities for energetic exercise was opened at Ben Rhydding, near Ilkley. Typically, Harrogate dithered over the new ideas but then, towards the end of the century, was persuaded of their economic value. Consequently, one or two 'hydros' were opened. In 1878, the Harrogate Hydropathic Company bought the *Swan Hotel*, one of the town's grandest, and equipped it with bathing

facilities that included a Turkish Bath. Among the large establishments that came into being in the 1890s were the Cairn Hydro and Harlow Manor Hydro.

Richard Ellis, one of the civic dignitaries who had been present when the Charter was received, loosened his purse strings for the benefit of the town. It was he who covered the cost of the Victoria Monument, in which a large statue of the Queen was installed under a slender Gothic spire. The Monument was unveiled in 1887, the year of the Queen's Golden Jubilee, by the Marquis of Ripon. At this time the Valley Gardens had just been created. The new Council acquired land between the Royal Pump Room and Bogs Field, creating storage reservoirs for the waters of the mineral springs. The land was laid out as a pleasure garden, complete with broad walkways and a bandstand.

Music-making formed a major part of the cultural life of Harrogate. In 1882, the Wood family of Heckmondwike moved into town. The head of the family was a tailor who also

94 The Cairn Hydropathic combined treatment with hotel facilities, *c.*1907.

95 *The Cairn Hotel* was originally the Cairn Hydropathic.

96 The Winter Garden, *The Cairn*.

97 An ox roasting on High Harrogate Stray to celebrate Queen Victoria's Jubilee, June 1887.

98 Valley Gardens and Pump Room in 1926.

played second viola in the theatre orchestra. The Woods formed their own choral society and parlour performances of great oratorios, including *Elijah* and *Messiah*. A talented son, Arthur, became 'solo boy' in the choir of St Peter's Church. When his voice broke, he turned to musical instruments, including piccolo and flute. On leaving school, aged 12, he became an errand boy to a hosier. A family friendship introduced him to the Spa Concert Rooms and to the musical world of the town. Arthur became an accomplished flautist and

pianist and was organist at the Presbyterian church, being paid £10 a year. When a Municipal Orchestra was formed in 1896, he became deputy to the conductor, J. Sydney Jones. As a solo pianist he played four times a day at concerts in the Valley Gardens for £2 10s. a week. He recalled to his daughter Lyn the cold Easter mornings when he wore mittens: the women had long skirts, huge busts, thin waists and marvellous hats with feathers; the men wore silk hats and frock coats. Arthur Wood left Harrogate to find fame and fortune

99 A social event at the Cheltenham Pump Room, 1853.

100 Bandstand in Valley Gardens.

101 *Left*. The old Concert Rooms *c*.1890.

102 *Below*. Royal Spa Concert Rooms and Gardens, which stood next to the Royal Hall, on the Cheltenham Estate, was built in 1835. It occupied six acres of land which included a boating lake and skating rink. It was demolished in 1939.

103 *Right*. Royal Spa Concert Rooms and *George Hotel*.

in the south but the Dale Country he loved was to be evoked by *My Native Heath*, a composition in four movements, named Barwick Green, Knaresborough Stattus, Ilkley Tarn and Bolton Abbey. (Barwick Green was to achieve considerable fame as the signature tune of the radio series *The Archers*.)

So far, Harrogate had kept out what some residents called 'the riff-raff'. The town was not beset by day-trippers, whose reputation was worse than their actions. The local newspaper, referring to occasional complaints, said their offences were usually confined to picking heather on Harlow Moor. One of the Commissioners, William Taylor, had remarked when the proposed incorporation of the town in 1883 had been discussed that, for all the talk of Harrogate's dependence on the gentry, it was the middle classes who had made

Harrogate what it was. The middle classes could maintain a genteel way of life because there existed a large reservoir of cheap labour to perform exacting manual tasks, from quarrying stone for the new buildings to attending the families as domestics. In the 1880s, about 2,000 domestic servants were employed, forfeiting high wages for the security and status such work was supposed to offer them. Other workers formed the staffs at large hotels. The shopworkers were expected to remain on their feet for long hours with little respite. Yet more workers maintained the transport system. Coal and most of the goods required by the town were now being brought in by rail, about 280 men being employed at the Starbeck sidings and attendant loco sheds. Railwaymen gave the better-off their high mobility.

104   Harlow Moor in the early 20th century.

Day-trippers helped to lubricate the economy. The clergy might have been expected to take a Christian attitude and show tolerance towards visitors but men such as the Rev. Horatio James, vicar of Christ Church, regarded them as being of no benefit to the town. Admittedly, his outcry came as he defended the holiness of the Sabbath. He had heard of a proposal by the Improvement Commissioners in 1863 to approach the North Eastern Railway in the hope of persuading them to operate a Sunday service (one train each way) between York and Harrogate. The vicar, invoking day-trippers en masse, said they annoyed the more respectable and regular visitors by their rude intrusion into every place. They also shocked the feelings of the more conscientious and devout. He asserted that regular visitors would be driven away altogether 'by the noise and shouting and smoking and profane jesting'. In 1892, the *Daily Graphic*, writing about Harrogate, considered that its absolute immunity from the ordinary tripper was a supreme advantage over many other holiday resorts. As we have seen, Harrogate was well served by the railway, and by 1892 it was possible for a Londoner to board a train at King's Cross at 9.45 a.m. and be in the spa town by 2.20 p.m. For a time, any wealthy holidaymaker who wished to take his horse-carriage to Harrogate could do so by rail, the town having a special loading bay and a suitable wagon. A writer in *Kelly's Directory* for 1889 asserted that Harrogate's recent expansion was due mainly to the provision of 'the great railway facilities between this town and the large manufacturing towns … enabling businessmen to reside here'.

The Victorian age was a time when curiosity about natural history and antiquities led to the formation of many urban-based organisations. At the *St George Inn*, Harrogate, on 5 August 1878, was founded the Bicycle Touring Club, the first cycling club in the world. By 1883, it had become the Cyclists' Touring Club and, as such, it has survived to the present day. The cyclists of Harrogate went

far and wide. One day, an excursion might take them to Fountains Abbey, a continually popular haunt, and another day they were in the Dale Country, stopping for tea and scones at the cottages and farmhouses that became recognised halts for cyclists. Others called at inns to imbibe something a little stronger.

Harrogate venerated the Queen. After 14 April 1887, when the foundation of the aforementioned Victoria Monument was laid, featuring a statue of the Queen sculpted by Webber, the sound of building work was heard on every hand. The Duke of Clarence was in town on 18 July 1889 to open an Infirmary, and Mr. Harry, Borough Engineer, and Drs. Oliver and Black were sent to various leading Continental spas to judge what Harrogate would need to match European practice. It was recommended that the Old Victoria Baths should be rebuilt. The Council pondered this for a few years, then suddenly and boldly, in the 1890s, decided to construct, on a lavish scale and at a cost estimated at £118,000, what was to become the Royal Baths. They were declared open by the Duke of Cambridge on 23 July 1897, the year when Queen Victoria celebrated her Diamond Jubilee. Visitors marvelled at the facilities. Water was pumped directly to the Baths from a number of springs. A peat bath was available. Seawater for a brine bath was transported by rail from Teesside. A choice of nearly forty different kinds of bath was available and treatments were offered for sufferers from gout, rheumatism, arthritis, sciatica, lumbago, skin disease, liver and kidney conditions.

The Duchy estate came into being when David Simpson, a councillor who was also a large-scale builder, purchased 54 prime acres from the Duchy of Lancaster. Here was created a grand suburb of large houses set in extensive grounds. The middle of the property was occupied by Duchy Road, the name commemorating an old association. Indeed, most of the houses were sold on Duchy leases of 99 years. In the early 1900s, some properties were

105 & 106 *Left*. A treatment room at the Royal Baths. *Right*. The great pump hall of the Royal Baths.

107 Intestinal douche room.

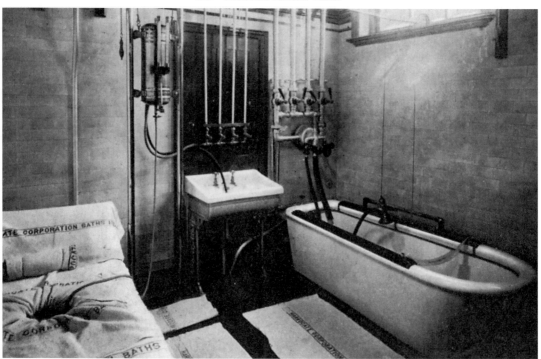

108   Dispensing waters from the circular counter at the Royal Baths caféteria.

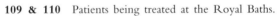

109 & 110   Patients being treated at the Royal Baths.

111   The stone-laying ceremony of the Royal Baths and Winter Gardens, 10 July 1894.

being let at a rent of between £40 and £75 a year.

In the spring of 1900, Samuel Stead, borough surveyor, retired after 11 vital years of office in a town with a greatly augmented population. Samuel's department originally consisted of himself and one assistant. By the time of his retirement he had three assistants, a writing clerk and an apprentice surveyor. He had been concerned with matters of hygiene, such as reconstructing the sewerage system and providing public toilets in Devonshire Place, Cold Bath Road and the Valley Gardens. He was involved in the purchase and redevelopment of what is now the Royal Baths estate, with the design of the aforementioned Valley

Gardens, and much besides. He was an industrious, uncomplaining public official, a man in the right place at the right time, who quite literally left his mark on the town. In the same year, Harrogate extended its bounds and created two new wards, Starbeck and Bilton. The extension increased the population by about 7,600 and brought in an additional £41,000 through the rates. Starbeck, which lay midway between Harrogate and Knaresborough, had its growth stimulated by the railway and had become an industrial centre, thought not on a grand scale. Here were industries of modest size, such as a sawing and moulding works, a corn mill powered by steam and a bottling plant for mineral water.

Chapter Seven

The Twentieth Century

The new century was marked by the opening of the Grand Opera House in Oxford Street. (It became the Harrogate Theatre.) At their first annual meeting, the board reported on a successful year and announced that all the shops on the ground-floor frontage had been let. That same year, the *Royal Hotel* was badly damaged by fire and, as a separate item of interest, the Borough Council decided to introduce peat bathing at the Montpellier Pump Room, an experience which a local man described in the *Harrogate Advertiser* as being 'rather erotic—it felt as if your body was being enveloped with quantities of hot velvet'. When the birthday of Queen Victoria (and also the Relief of Mafeking by British forces) were celebrated in Harrogate, the event was reported in the *Advertiser* of 2 May at considerable length. 'Street after street were swathed with dense bunting, coloured flags and patriotic mottoes. The more important public buildings were also festooned with gas devices ... In the evening there was a great banquet at the *Queen's Hotel*.' Alderman Fortune, referring to 'mere southern Spas', noted that in 1899 Harrogate had more sunshine than Bournemouth, Brighton or Hastings.

On 18 July 1900, a vast new hotel aptly named *Majestic* had a ceremonial opening. When they pondered over the plans, which bore affinities to those for the house of a nobleman, the council were concerned that it would be too close to the old sulphur well. Trial borings were made and three councillors,

including the mayor, gave it the sniff test for half an hour but did not detect the familiar 'rotten egg' tang of sulphur. The *Majestic* stood out from the older buildings, having been fashioned from brick rather than gritstone. It was rumoured (falsely) that the hotel would have been built of stone if masons had not gone on strike, and (more likely) that the foundations alone absorbed one million bricks. The workers had enough leisure-time for hard-drinking and for cricket, forming their own team, the activities of which were reported in the local newspaper. Rumours abounded. The hotel, majestic in every sense, rose on the Springbank estate, which had come onto the market following the death of Nicholas Carter, one-time mayor. The purchaser, Sir Blundell Maple of Frederick Hotels, is said to have stayed at *The Queen*, then regarded as the best hotel in town, and was miffed at the attitude of the manager when he complained about some aspect of his bill. He left the hotel determined to build one of such magnificence it would put *The Queen* out of business, and he was not in a joking mood.

His *Majestic* was vast and opulent. Built at a cost of a quarter of a million pounds, it had accommodation for 400 guests. Anyone who toured the hotel found their lower jaw drooping with astonishment at a dining room adorned by palms and illuminated by chandeliers, a silk-panelled ballroom for 500 dancers, and a 'smoking' room decorated with elaborate 16th-century carvings brought from an Egyptian palace that had become a trophy of war. At the heart of the hotel was the Winter Garden, the largest glazed interior in Yorkshire, the floor space extending to 8,000 square feet. The *Harrogate Advertiser* described it as a 'delicious retreat' but so large that 'visitors can, on wet days, enjoy their usual walk under the most happy conditions'. To the *Majestic* came Prince Henry of Prussia, whose brother was the Emperor of Germany. He had originated the idea of an Anglo-German motor tour of Britain. The Maharaja of Patiala took over an entire floor of the hotel.

With Harrogate thriving, Alderman David Simpson, a former mayor and developor of the Duchy estate, built a rival to the *Majestic* in a field that overlooked the Valley Gardens. Known as the *Spa Grand Hotel*, and opened on 23 May 1903, it had six domes compared with the *Majestic*'s one. The hotel's name was later changed to *Grand Hotel*; it closed down just after the Second World War.

Edwardian Days

Queen Victoria died in 1901, but the drive and optimism of the Victorian period endured throughout the reign of Edward VII, ending abruptly with the First World War, which robbed the land of its youngest and finest and shattered the old social distinctions. The statue of Victoria—Our Lady of the Spa, in the words of a local historian—continued to keep watch on Harrogate from her perch on the Jubilee monument. For anyone with the means and inclination for enjoyment, Harrogate was a good place in which to live. The spa town was developed so rapidly, with imposing Victorian houses standing in broad avenues, it was being compared with the Klondike.

A local celebrity, Alderman Charles Fortune (who would be distinguished by having an inn named after him), saw the Royal Baths through to completion and extended the waterworks. He was also the man who saw the Kursaal completed, though on a less grand scale

112 The *Majestic Hotel*.

113 One of the entrants of
the German-British motor tour
passing the *Majestic* in July 1911.

114 Fire at the *Majestic Hotel*
on 20 June 1924.

115 Demolition of the
Winter Garden and Conser-
vatory at the *Majestic Hotel* in
1972.

116   Westmorland Street, decorated for the Coronation of Edward VII in 1902.

117   J. Brown's Saddlers in Oxford Street, taken during the Coronation of Edward VII.

118 Station Square.

119 Station Square during the First World War, with the Victoria monument which dates from the 1887 Jubilee.

than had been originally proposed. It was to have been capable of seating 3,000 people, with supporting rooms and halls, but the size was reduced to accommodate an audience of 1,200. The foundation stone was laid by Alderman Simpson on 1 January 1902. It was set well back from a busy Ripon Road. The hall was opened by Sir Hubert Parry on 4 January in the following year. Appearing at the hall in the early years were such luminaries as Sarah Bernhardt, Clara Butt, Lily Langtry, Fritz Kreisler, George Robey and Nellie Melba. The composer Edward Elgar was a notable visitor to Harrogate who would feel at home at the Kursaal; he had visited Germany, where his music was greatly appreciated.

Local government had begun to function with vigour and courage, while retaining its Yorkshire common sense. From time to time, some ratepayers would remind the Council that costs were becoming unacceptably high. In 1902, plans to replace the Royal Pump Room and introduce an electric tramway system to

Harrogate were left 'lying on the table'. Yet a new sewage disposal scheme was inaugurated in 1903, and 1906 was notable for the opening of a new library in Victoria Avenue, three-quarters of the total cost of rather more than £10,000 being a gift from Andrew Carnegie, whose name was writ large on the building. The idea of building a new Town Hall next to the library was not the type of scheme for which special loan sanction had been obtained in one of the Acts of Parliament the corporation had promoted, so it was put to a public meeting—and voted down.

During the first quarter of the 20th century, Harrogate's fame as a spa town took on an international character. The Harrogate season, hitherto from July to September, to allow for the London social season and for grouse-shooting in Yorkshire and Scotland, became spread throughout the year. The town improved its medical services and provided visitors with a wide range of entertainment. By 1911, it had 800 shops of various kinds

120   Crescent Gardens from the Kursaal.

121 The Kursaal, on the left, where great artistes such as Pavlova, Bernhardt and Melba performed before the First World War.

122 The Carnegie Library which dates from 1906.

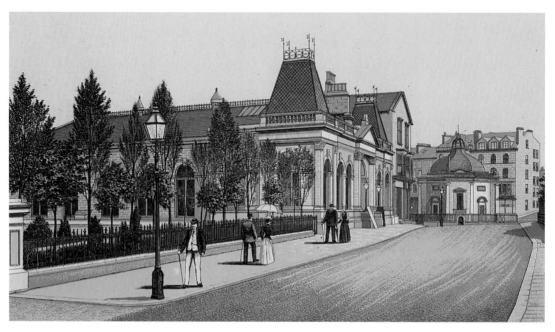

123   The old Town Hall which is now the Mercer Art Gallery.

and, as a shopping and marketing centre, 'had the edge' on old-time Knaresborough. The population of the borough was now 33,703; boosted by the families of businessmen who commuted to Leeds and Bradford. Among the parallel developments was a number of boarding schools. The town's housing stock was numbered in thousands, including mini-mansions and capacious terraced houses. In 1912, Lloyd George upset the townsfolk by a remark made during a parliamentary speech: 'Even Harrogate has slums.'

In Edwardian times, the visitor who had means, leisure and medical advice went through a by-now-hallowed routine of rising early and taking a pre-breakfast stroll to the Royal Pump Room, where the water was consumed as the doctor ordered. He or she would then have another languid stroll, perhaps taking in the Crescent Gardens, where a band was playing or, if the weather was inclement, in the winter gardens or the promenades at the Kursaal. Back at the hotel, breakfast was at eight, and the visitor withdrew to his or her rooms for a while to

wait for the purgative effects of the waters. Friends taking a mid-morning stroll met each other, compared ailments, updated themselves with local gossip and patronised Harrogate's fabulous range of exclusive shops, where they were fussed over by large staffs. The nobility would expect to have stock taken to their hotels, where they might select what they needed in private. Souvenirs were purchased, the principal reminder of a holiday in Harrogate being a family photograph. It is said that when a maharaja and his family who were staying at the Cairn Hydro had their 'likeness' taken by a local photographer, the instructions were that the photographs should be packed in crates—with a plentiful amount of rose petals. After lunch, horse-drawn vehicles were available to convey the wealthy visitors to a beauty spot such as the former Cistercian abbey of Fountains, in the valley of the Skell, near Ripon. The evening might be spent dancing at a ball organised at one of the large hotels. Those who were stiff-limbed with age might prefer an evening spent at the Opera House or the Empire Theatre.

124 Lowly Harrogate. These shops used to stand in the yard of the *Ship* inn before their demolition *c.*1900.

125 Nydd Vale Terrace enhanced by flags and bunting on a national occasion.

126 & 127 Promenading in Crescent Gardens and the plaque with the Festival Pavilion in the background, showing 'Cupid & Psyche' by the Italian master Giovanni Maria Benzoni.

Thirsty Harrogate had its water supply augmented by the construction of reservoirs at Scargill and Roundhill, but there was the usual procrastination over developing the (over-crowded) Royal Pump Room. Should it be replaced by a grand structure or simply modified to permit greater use? Those who feared that a heavy structure would somehow interfere with the flow of sulphur water managed to fight off the prospect of a neo-baroque structure, and a small annexe was added to the existing graceful building.

On a cloudy October day in 1910 the foundation stone of what was to become a palatial range of buildings in Pennypot Lane was laid. Queen Ethelburga's College would become an outstanding example of a public school developed in the 20th century. The chapel, like much else, was a gift from Lord Mountgarret. At the laying of the foundation stone, the trowel was wielded by Dr. Cosmo Gordon Lang, who was then Archbishop of York, and the completed premises were opened on 27 September 1912 by the Duchess of Albany, using a gold key. At the first Speech Day, Miss Body, headmistress and founder of

Queen Margaret's School, reminded a large assembly that it was also Trafalgar Day 'and spoke of what that meant to England'. (Queen Ethelburga's College is today at Thorpe Underwood Hall, York, where it has an impressive range and quality of facilities.)

In the golden summer of 1911, the Harrogate Municipal Orchestra, conducted by Julian Clifford, gave the first provincial performance of Elgar's Second Symphony. Sir Edward Elgar himself was in town the following year, and in a memorable concert conducted his *Imperial March*, the concert overture *In the South*, *Enigma Variations*, *Chanson de Nuit* and the *Wand of Youth* suite. Elgar was a regular visitor to Harrogate during the first three decades of the last century, and he conducted concerts in the Kursaal. Details of the celebrated composer-conductor's habit of taking a daily walk when at Harrogate were recorded by H.H. Walker, who tried to pluck up courage to acquire Elgar's autograph. He once trailed the composer from the *Hotel Majestic*, across Crescent Gardens and into Valley Gardens.

The climactic year for Harrogate socially was 1911 when, on a single day in August, three eminent dowagers were present. These were Queen Alexandra, the Empress Marie of Russia (her sister), and Queen Amelie of Portugal. Other royals who graced Harrogate that season were Princess Victoria, Prince Henry of Prussia (brother to the Kaiser) and Prince Christopher of Greece, with the normal gathering of aristocrats and maharajas. Some of the visitors were to be remembered for their outlandish behaviour. Lord and Lady Charles Beresford were at the *Majestic* for the Season in 1912. Her Ladyship, doubtless peeved by her husband's philandering, was boorish and also unsociable—until she heard that Elgar was about to arrive in Harrogate and would be staying at the hotel. She sent her car to meet him and they were companions at dinner that night. Writing to a family friend, Lady Alice Stuart Wortley, Elgar reported that she loathed Harrogate and its people, and added:

> Of course, Harrogate thinks itself very fashionable & more than a little chic, & the ladies dress up terribly. Lady C shews her contempt for the whole thing by wearing a hat at dinner & and curious sack-like robe … We left the Dining Room and went into one of the salons—somebody began to sing. Whereupon Lady C uttered a shriek and we fled!

The entrance to the Valley Gardens was given a more imposing appearance in 1912. Until then, visitors entered by a small wooden gate that was flanked by wooden palings. The Council's Stray and Pleasure Grounds Committee asked the Borough Surveyor to plan something more spacious and elegant, and a crescent of land was set aside for the tables and chairs that were to be used by those visiting the Pump Room to drink the waters. In June, the Lord Mayor of London, Sir David Burnett, opened an annexe to the Royal Pump Room after being driven through the town in the state landau, brought specially from London, and before a vast crowd in the winter gardens he amused local people by declaring that Harrogate was not a seaside resort, and that 'despite the growing number of requests for hotel rooms having a view of the sea … the town was clearly destined to be known as the Queen of *Inland* watering places.' At a banquet for Sir David and 400 guests at the *Majestic*, Sir David's speech indicated he had been well primed about local matters. He thought the people of Harrogate would be foolish to hand over their splendid natural and national assets to private enterprise:

> At one time the baths and wells were a hobby costing the ratepayers £2,000 a year. They were now so profitable that during the past eight years over £75,000 had been paid in redemption of loans and interest, while the rates have been relieved by the handsome sum of £11,500.

Having dined, the company strolled through the hotel gardens and into those of the Kursaal and Spa Rooms. Darkness had been banished by the normal lighting and an array of Chinese

128 A procession to the memorial service at Harrogate following the death of King Edward VII.

129 The Brooklands to Harrogate air-race, 22 July 1911, landed on the Stray between the Leeds and Wetherby roads.

130 Reconstructed well heads in Valley Gardens.

lanterns. The fountains were operating and above the chatter of people music could be heard. Waltzes by Strauss and Lehar were interspersed with a more contemporary sound—that of American ragtime.

In the pre-1914 period, visitors had an astonishingly wide choice of musical entertainment, ranging from concerts and recitals to the hurdy-gurdy and barrel organ that provided music in the street. Residential musicians performed at the big hotels, and groups such as Otto Schwartz and his Bavarian String Band could be heard beside Pier Head or in the Valley Gardens. It was claimed by local doctors

that the fresh air of Harrogate was enough to cure the physical and mental depression that was a consequence of urban life and little exercise, as well as what was defined as 'brain fag', otherwise known as overwork. The bath-chair of Victorian times, as adapted by Tom Rochford to be driven by pedal power, took the weight off the legs of those with the leisure and means to hire a man who described himself in a local directory as the 'Bath Chair Man'. Tom was able to sit as well as pedal as he took his distinguished clients for a ride. When his passenger was Princess Alex of Hesse (who married the Russian Tsar and would be murdered by the Bolsheviks in 1918) they had company in the form of a bicycle-riding detective. A longer outing ended by the six-acre lake in a setting of weather-eroded gritstone known as Plumpton Rocks. The scene had been painted by J.M.W. Turner and Girton, and was rendered as an oil painting by William Mellow, a resident of Harrogate, in the 1890s.

In 1913 the *Harrogate Advertiser* was effusive about the status of Harrogate as a premier spa town: 'There are many thousands of people in England who regularly turn their eyes to Harrogate. Their yearly visit to this famous Spa is the one thing that must never be omitted or postponed. Harrogate has become the vogue, not because it has practically every treatment to offer that any single Spa on the Continent can boast, but because the people who flock here seldom if ever leave disappointed.'

Two World Wars

The fripperies of the Edwardian period were followed by the grim realities of the First World War. At the time Harrogate was feeling pleased with itself, having a population of about 35,000 and a housing stock numbering over 8,000. No less than 75,000 visitors had used its facilities. Now, on a wave of patriotism, young men queued to enrol at a recruiting office in Raglan Street, many to don khaki and serve in the 5th West Yorkshire Volunteers (the 'Harrogate Pals'). The German name Kursaal, for the concert hall, was changed to Royal Hall, though no one thought to remove the original name from the stonework. For Edward Elgar, it was an especially poignant time. There was no doubting his patriotism, but he had many good German friends and it was in that land that his music had first been widely appreciated. An avid writer of letters, he wrote

131   The Lord Mayor of London in Station Square, 8 June 1913.

132   Low Harrogate in 1903 and the touring band of Otto Schwarz.

to Alice Caroline Stuart Wortley in 1917, when the war was dragging wearily on:

> Oh! this weather & I was dreaming yesterday of woods & fields & perhaps a little drive round Harrogate—or a little play journey to Fountains or some lovely remembrance of long ago idylls, & now—deep snow. Well, I have put it all in my music & also much more that has never happened.

During the war, St Mary's Church, designed by Samuel Chapman, was opened in Low Harrogate. Chapman had already made a mark on the town with the design for the Royal Bath Hospital. St Mary's replaced an earlier structure that, considered unsafe, had been demolished in 1904. The material from this demolition was re-cycled to provide Harrogate Ladies College with a chapel. In the closing stages of the war, an influenza epidemic spread through the land and Harrogate was not spared the infection.

After the war was over, something of the former way of life was revived at Harrogate. For the more active visitors, there was the early morning drink of sulphur water, followed by a leisurely walk from the Pump Room to the Crescent Gardens (where music was played by a small orchestra) and to the Valley Gardens, where older visitors would include those trying to recapture the spirit of the halcyon years of the Edwardian period. In the late morning, it was fashionable to visit the Winter Gardens and listen to a concert provided by the municipal orchestra. For ex-servicemen, especially those whose lives had been shattered by incessant trench warfare, Harrogate represented fresh air, treatment for their ailments and the blessed gift of rest. Bettys Café and Tea Rooms were established in 1919 (to be moved to its present premises in Parliament Street, adjoining Montpellier Parade, in 1976).

Harrogate's spa town activity continued. Visitors included many well-to-do folk with chauffered cars which had little competition from other vehicles on roads that still saw the passage of horse-drawn carts. In 1923, the Ladies College brought its new chapel into use. Elsewhere, Bogs Field, with its numerous mineral wells, was tidied up. The wells were delineated by brick shafts, and each was kept airtight by means of a wax-impregnated wooden cover that rose and fell with fluctuations of the water, providing an airtight seal. The provision of tennis courts and a paddling pool ran against the spirit of the acts that governed The Stray. In December 1926, Harrogate featured in the headlines of national newspapers, when Agatha Christie (1890-1976), the celebrated author, who was missing from home, turned up at the *Swan Hydro* (now *Old Swan Hotel*). This incident, trivial in the context of the Harrogate story, did the town no harm. The publicity value was (and is) enormous. Various theories, including overwork, the recent death of her mother, and marital problems, were all put forward to account for the distinguished author's disappearance and apparent memory loss. Her choice of Harrogate was made when she saw a poster at Waterloo Station in London advertising the spa town. She stayed at the *Swan*

under the assumed name of Theresa Neele, her husband's mistress. At that time, the rate at the hotel was £5 10s. a week.

For the writer, it was an enjoyable time. While over 1,000 policemen and civilians were searching for the distinguished author of 'who-dunnits', she was enjoying the high life, with other guests, at dances, balls and palm court entertainment. The search for Agatha was the first missing person inquiry in which aircraft were used. After 10 days, Bob Tappin, a banjo player at the hotel, recognised her and alerted the police. Colonel Christie, her husband, arrived to collect her. She kept him waiting for half an hour in the lounge while she finished dressing for dinner and the couple had an affectionate reunion before enjoying a meal. But after only two years, the couple were divorced, and Colonel Christie married—Theresa Neele. Agatha also re-married, was made a Dame Commander of the British Empire in 1971, and wrote prolifically until her death five years later. (The strange story of the disappearing authoress was re-told in 1977 in a film called *Agatha*, starring Vanessa Redgrave and Dustin Hoffman. The film was shot on location at the *Old Swan Hotel* and in Harrogate.)

The town returned to a more humdrum way of life. In the summer of 1927, the general manager of the Royal Baths had a fact-finding tour on the continent and concluded, to everyone's satisfaction, that Harrogate was holding its own as a spa town. At home, an alderman complained about the hosts of day-trippers that 'flood the Valley Gardens to the exclusion of those here for the cure'. Harrogate's prospering public enterprises needed every support following the international trade slump of 1929. Profitable enterprises sank into deficit and debt, though, when the British Spas' Federation published a report in 1929 that showed all but one of the eight top British spas were recording an annual loss, Harrogate noted with a measure of relief that it was the exception. Against £39,371 spent there was set an income of only £41,113.

133 Royal Hall and Parliament Street.

134   Terriers leaving Harrogate on 5 August 1914.

Harrogate's decline as a spa came when the 'iron' tablet succeeded the time-honoured practice of 'taking the waters' and lotions and ointments were found to be more agreeable than bathing in sulphur water. In 1930, the Victoria Baths were closed, to be remodelled into council offices. The Municipal Orchestra was disbanded. The Pump Room, for long a profitable enterprise, began to lose money, and the Royal Baths returned a substantial loss. The Borough Council fought back and in 1933 built a Sun Pavilion and Sun Colonnade, with a combined length of 600 ft., along the north side of the Valley Gardens, a popular scheme that was opened by Lord Horder. In the Sun Pavilion, special glass filtered out any harmful solar radiation. The former Winter Gardens in the Royal Baths became an updated Lounge Hall and Fountains Court. That same year, when the Council decided to deck the West Park Stray with flower beds and shrubberies, irate residents formed a Stray Defence Association.

The shops of Harrogate continued to attract a quality clientele, including Queen Mary who, while staying at Harewood House, made a point of looking at antique shops. When something took her fancy, the Queen did not always insist on paying for it. The owner was unlikely to press his claim. The old market burnt down in 1937 but had been replaced two years later. Harrogate's bus station, opened in 1938, occupied a spacious site beside the central railway station and was handy to the main taxi rank. It formalised a trend that began just before the First World War, when charabancs and buses used the station yard. When, in 1935, the West Yorkshire Road Car Company, provider of local bus services, bought the Belvedere estate at the corner of Victoria Avenue and West Park, it was their intention to adapt the former home of Lord Faber into offices and to use the large garden at the rear as a bus station. Instead, a site near the railway station was developed, a row of railway

135 & 136 St Mary's Church was built in 1825 to serve the Low Harrogate area. It was replaced in 1916.

137 Miss Elizabeth Jones (with the parasol) and her staff. She was headmistress of Harrogate Ladies College between 1898 and 1914.

138 Harrogate Ladies College on its 90th anniversary in 1983.

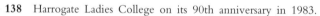

139 Crescent Gardens in May 1910 and the proclamation of George V outside the Royal Baths.

140 A band playing in the Royal Baths' Gardens in 1916.

141   Parliament Street in the horse and cart days.

workers' cottages in lower Station Parade being demolished to provide a yard of 3,538 square yards. The bus station opened on 1 July 1938. The red-painted buses of the West Yorkshire company became a cheery sight in the town.

In 1939, the Royal Baths were extended and the demolition men moved into the old Spa Rooms, which had become neglected and redundant. Their place was taken by the Sun Pavilion and Lounge Hall. The octagonal Pump Room, which for many years had represented the old Harrogate, was used as a store, but was to have a fleeting period of celebrity as a municipal restaurant until, in 1953, it was re-opened as a museum telling the story of the Spa. Harrogate became a run-down place, with something like one-sixth of the houses on the Duchy of Lancaster estate, one of the best areas in town, being vacant.

The Second World War was the proverbial blessing in disguise. When hostilities began, large numbers of civil servants were evacuated to the town, to be quartered at the big hotels, which became office blocks, the workers becoming known as 'guinea pigs' because they paid a guinea a week in rent. Some of them remained permanently. As an example of the upsurge of population, the Post Office Savings Bank employed about 1,200 people. The Admiralty occupied *The Royal* and the Air Ministry Equipment Section was based on *The Crown* and *Harlow Manor Hydro*. *The Old Swan* became a branch of the Ministry of Aircraft Production and the Ministry of Supply. Harlow Hill Tower, built in 1829, was brought into use as a post for observing passing aircraft, especially those of the enemy. Harrogate's only air raid occurred on 12 September 1940, when there was a daylight attack by a lone German bomber, a Junker 88, which dived towards the vast bulk of the *Majestic*, thought (erroneously, as it turned out) to house the offices of a department of the Air Ministry, and released three bombs. The first, which did not explode,

142 Unveiling the War Memorial on 1 September 1923.

became lodged in the hotel itself. The second bomb fell in the grounds of the hotel. The third demolished a villa standing at the corner of Swan and Ripon roads, also fracturing gas and water mains. The unexploded bomb was found standing upright in an upstairs room; soldiers looking for it had at first mistaken it for a water tank. The men removed the bomb using one of the hotel lifts. When the bomb had been rendered safe, the casing was used to raise money for the Harrogate Spitfire Fund. Captured German documents revealed the enemy had believed it was a worthwhile target, but a popular newspaper claimed, at the time of the raid, that the pilot was on a revenge attack: he had been refused a place in the restaurant when he had called there in 1938.

Modern Days

The Royal Pump Room, closed after the war, was re-opened as a museum in 1953 and its exhibits tell the story of the Spa. A visitor might taste sulphur water, which is bitter and sharp, either inside the museum or from an outside tap. Since 1950, Harrogate has been advertised as 'Britain's Floral Resort' and has been the venue for the Northern Antique Dealers' Fair, held in September at the Royal Baths Assembly Rooms. In 1952, when Arnold Kellett became a local teacher, he was just in time to witness the terminal stages of a dying spa. As he wrote, 'The stately Queen of the Inland Watering Places was painlessly slipping away into history.' In 1953, Bill Baxter, the borough publicity manager, made 'twinning' arrangements with Luchon in the French Pyrenees (another spa) and set a pattern of 'twinning' which was to become general throughout the land. In 1959, a temporary exhibition hall was erected on the Spa Rooms Gardens and the modern role of the town as a major centre for conferences and exhibitions was established. It was a timely move, for in 1968 the Leeds Regional Hospital Board, which used the facilities of the Royal Baths for the treatment of rheumatism, terminated its contract

with Harrogate Corporation. In the following year, the Royal Baths closed for treatment though the Turkish Baths remain.

In spring, The Stray nowadays burgeons with flowering daffodils and crocuses and the Prince of Wales roundabout becomes a colourful garden. The Montpellier Gardens are colourful for most of the year. At Harlow Carr, beyond the Valley Gardens and the pinewoods, is the trial station of the Northern Horticultural Society, developed in the 1950s on 26 acres of land leased from the Borough Council, 18 acres being taken up by woodland. Some claimed it to be the last hardy remnant of the historic Forest of Knaresborough. The deposits of leaf mould were an ideal site for such as rhododendrons and azaleas. The Princess Royal, of Harewood House, gave to the Northern Horticultural Society a strain of blue primrose and also planted a commemorative tree. The Society now has over 10,000 members and Harlow Carr gardens are visited by over 100,000 people annually. Their evolution continues. Six full-time gardeners attend to 68 acres, and among the projects are new herb and fruit gardens. A Millennium Appeal has been launched to raise money for a five-year garden development plan. Over half a million pounds was spent on a new restaurant, proposals for the old restaurant including its development as an education and training facility.

During the 1960s, those who sat and sipped mineral waters in the Grand Pump Room of the Royal Baths might reflect on a frieze of words taken from a poem by James Montgomery, who had visited the town in 1825: 'Then in life's goblet freely press/The leaves that give it bitterness.' In 1961, the town seemed to throb with life and vitality. A vicar referred to its cosmopolitan population and noted it was fast-changing. Some 900 names appeared on the electoral roll of the church. 'Each year we take off about 100 names of residents who have died or moved and we add 100 names of newcomers to the town. And that's a lot!' Since the 1951 census, the

143 A horse-drawn bus run by Robert Dent between Harrogate and New Park, *c.*1900.

144 Taxicabs outside New Victoria Baths, May 1908.

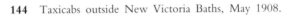

145 Railway houses associated with the old Bruswick Station. They form part of West End Avenue.

146 The tap from which sulphur water can be drawn. It protudes from the side of the Royal Pump Museum.

population had grown from 50,400 to 56,300, an increase of 11.6 per cent, which was one of the largest in the country outside the new towns. Included in that increase were those who came to Harrogate when the Borough Council set out to persuade large firms to establish their administrative centres here. The first 'big fish', landed in 1953, was the ICI Fibres Division headquarters, the workplace of about 1,500 top scientists. To Harrogate came the Dunlopillo Division of the Dunlop Rubber Company (1,000 people, including a subsidiary), the Mercantile Credit Company (250 people) and the Regional Hospital Board.

Amazingly, this large-scale influx of big business did not noticeably change the gracious face of the town or destroy its value as a residential area for the industrial West Riding. In the five years up to 1961, about 1,800 private houses were built and the trend showed no signs of abating. Luxury flats were built in the Park Place area, each flat costing about £7,500. Amid the changes, some Harrogate businesses have retained an old-time flavour of quality service at a personal level. Among them is

147 Indoor palms at the Royal Baths.

148 Harrogate decorated for the Coronation celebrations of 1953.

149 The Harrogate Symphony Orchestra in 1920.

150   Summer crowd at the Royal Baths in July 1938.

151 Harlow Manor Hydro was built in 1875 and opened as a hydro in 1893.

Allens, the outfitters in Parliament Street, a firm founded by William Grover Allen who had arrived in town as a youth in the days when High and Low Harrogate were separated by green fields and when walkers passed through turnstiles to get from one to the other. The shop contains solid mahogany fittings and features a sweeping staircase. The jewellery firm of James R. Ogden & Sons was one of those which came into being during the town's Victorian heyday. When Marshall & Snelgrove had moved into fashionable James Street in 1906, Ogdens took a short tenancy of No. 38 before moving to larger premises in the same street. In the 1960s, Messrs. Busby extended their department store—a store which is now but a memory. By 1967, the rail system at Harrogate had shrunk to the extent that the town was served only by trains from York and Leeds. Industrial estates to the south and east give the town a modern aspect.

The Spring Flower Show, a 'hardy annual', was first held in the Valley Gardens in 1927. In the 1950s, when I chatted with William Bishop, Parks Superintendent, he told me that so diverse was the plant population

locally that 'we are approaching the botanical gardens stage'. Another objective was to achieve natural beauty and he was proud of the beautiful and uncommon plants growing in the Valley Gardens. Many were closely associated with Reginald Farrer, a great Yorkshire botanist, pioneer rock gardener, and collector of plants in far distant lands. In 1996, the Spring Flower Show was moved from the Valley Gardens to a 22-acre site on the Great Yorkshire showground and now caters for up to 55,000 visitors. Eighty-five per cent of the exhibits are under cover, so the show is no longer vulnerable to bad weather. Visitors see an unrivalled display of spring and early summer blooms, from daffodils to sweet peas and from pelargoniums to carnations, brought by amateur and professional growers.

In 1966, the Harrogate International Festival began life with the help of composer Benjamin Britten. A registered charity, its aim was to mirror events that had been enjoyed in the spa town's heyday. From the start, it attracted first-class artistes. By the early 1990s, however, the Festival, which takes place over a period of 17 days, had fallen victim, along with other regional festivals, to the cutbacks in Arts Council subsidies. To broaden its appeal, new strands were added, including jazz, comedy and street theatre, as well as community events for which there was no admission charge. Today, corporate sponsorship accounts for about 35 per cent of turnover. Over half of the 40,000 annual visitors to the Festival are from outside the Harrogate area.

The Great Yorkshire Show is in terms of scale and support the most notable county event. Once nomadic, a 100-acre permanent show-ground, just off the Wetherby road at Harrogate, was acquired in 1950. When F.M. Baldwin had been appointed secretary of the Yorkshire Agricultural Society in 1947, one of his first tasks was to buy and establish the event

at Harrogate. Doom was forecast by some but entries greatly increased, attendances rose and what had been a grass farm became, in relatively short time, one of the finest agricultural showgrounds in Europe. When, in 1957, the Great Yorkshire Show became a centenarian, the Society was visited by the Queen and the Duke of Edinburgh. In the year 2000, the Great Yorkshire Show was held on its permanent showground for the 50th time. In recent years, over £10 million has been spent on modernising and restructuring the ground. The first show of the new millennium cost £1.5 million to stage and was attended by over 120,000 people. Fifty years ago, the show attracted just over 300 stands, a number that has now risen to about a thousand. Once again,

152 Continental folk groups dancing on the Stray in 1988.

153   Wedderburn Ladies' Tea Club (from the Bertram Unne collection).

154   Harrogate Spring Flower Show in 1983.

155   Harrogate International Centre is one of Europe's finest conference and exhibition centres which includes a 2,000-seat auditorium and eight adjoining exhibition halls.

the Yorkshire Agricultural Society at Harrogate was acting as an important link between those whose livelihood is derived from the land and the urban folk who are their principal customers.

Harrogate has its Antique and Fine Art Fair, a magnet for some 10,000 visitors, towards the end of April. The Antiques Fair, a notable springtime event, has been held locally for over a quarter of a century. About £5 million-worth of desirable objects are displayed on stands that have room settings. At the latest fair, visitors stared hard and long at a victory wreath containing hair snipped from the head of the Duke of Wellington in 1844.

The far-sighted corporation has transformed Harrogate into a major conference centre, devising a state-of-the-art conference hall that was, in its time, as controversial as is the London Millennium Dome today. A vast circular edifice, the brick-built International Centre, with adjacent hotel, now gives Harrogate a modern look and facilities. The Centre is truly impressive. The main focal point for anyone entering is a circular reception desk situated in the middle of the foyer that provides telephone and paging facilities. A spiralling walkway passes through the bar and lounge areas into an auditorium with seating for 2,000 people which is overlooked by six interpreters'

156   The Doctor Visits Harrowgate, an early print of the wells.

booths. The first major event to be held at the Centre was the 1982 Eurovision Song Contest. There are currently seven interlinked exhibition halls, with a new one added in the year 2000. The Royal Hall, a decorative building of the early 20th century, has an ongoing restoration programme as part of the grand scheme.

In the Harrogate District are over 5,000 bed spaces available in hotels and guest houses alone. It is estimated that during 1998 the Harrogate District attracted 3.22 million business and holiday visitors, representing 6.67 million visitor days and resulting in a direct financial benefit of over £178 million. Some 7,000 jobs are related to this trade. The town evolved from mineral wells but the Council 'capped' the celebrated Tewit Well on The Stray in 1971 and four centuries of public access to its waters came to a close. A stone canopy dignifies the area but no one knows the precise location of the well that was at the foundation of Harrogate's good fortune.

Bibliography

Cooper, Lettice, *Yorkshire West Riding* (Hale, 1950)

Harrogate Advertiser

Haythornthwaite, W., *Harrogate Story* (Dalesman, 1954)

Hogg, Garry, *Blind Jack of Knaresborough* (Phoenix House, 1967)

Jennings, Bernard (ed.), *A History of Nidderdale* (Nidderdale History Group, 1967)

Jennings, Bernard (ed.), *A History of Harrogate and Knaresborough* (Harrogate WEA, 1970)

Kellett, Arnold, *Countryside Walks around Harrogate* (Dalesman, 1984)

Kellett, Arnold, *Harrogate: A Practical Guide for Visitors* (Dalesman, 1991)

Kennedy, Carol, *Harewood* (Hutchinson, 1982)

Muir, Richard, *The Dales of Yorkshire* (Macmillan, 1991)

Neesam, Malcolm G., *Exclusively Harrogate* (Smith Settle, 1989)

Neesam, Malcolm G., *Hotel Majestic* (Paramount Hotels, 2000)

Pill, David, *Yorkshire: The West Riding* (Batsford, 1977)

Pontefract, Ella, and Hartley, Marie, *Yorkshire Tour* (Dent, 1939)

Reid, Mark, *Harrogate* (Dalesman, 2000)

Rothwell, Catherine, *Around Harrogate* (Sutton, 1997)

Speakman, Colin, *Portrait of North Yorkshire* (Hale, 1986)

Thorpe's Illustrated Guide to Harrogate (Ackrill, 1886)

Vale, Edmund, *North Country* (Batsford, 1937)

Index

Illustration page numbers are printed in **bold** type

HARROGATE
1849

Killinghall Moor

Jenny Plain

Iron Gate Bridge

Harrogate End or Hill Top

Smithy Hill
High Harrogate National Training School

Grove House

Devonshire

Spring Bank

Swan Hotel

Royal Cheltenham Pump.
Promenade Room

Low Harrogate

Wesleyan Methodist Chapel

Central Harrogate

Beulah Place

Montpellier Public Baths

Mount Pleasant

Rock Cottages
Cornwall House

Spring Cottage

Prospect Cottage

Prospect Hill

British Foreign

Hopewell House

Independent Chapel

Harrogate

Bath Hospital

Baths

Wellington Terrace
Kensington Place

St Mary's Church
The Curacy

Green Farm
Farrahs Villa

Black Bogs

Binns Hole

Brunswick Terrace

Leeds Terrace

The Parsonage

Highwood Terrace
Commercial Inn

Quarry

Somerset House

Diamond House

Wood Cottage

Clarendon Hotel
Stone Pillars

York Place

Brunswick Hotel

THE STRAY

White House

Direction Post
The Cross Roads
Harrogate Station

Harlow House

Cold Bath

Lewis Well Chapel

New Inn

Harlow Cottage

Direction Post

Lodge

Harrogate Tunnel

Harlow Hill Tower
or the Observatory

Harlow Hill

Harlow Hill Quarries
Sandstone

Harlow Inn

Travellers Inn

Direction Post

Blythe Nook

Boundary Stone

Rossett Moor

Direction Post

Reproduced from the Ordnance Survey Map YORKSHIRE 154 *Surveyed in 1849 by Capt. Tucker R.E.*